MW00781349

HAUNTED HOUSES

HAUNTED HOUSES

Guide to
Spooky, Creepy, and Strange Places
across the USA

DANIEL DIEHL
and MARK P. DONNELLY

STACKPOLE
BOOKS

Copyright © 2010 by Daniel Diehl and Mark P. Donnelly

Published by
STACKPOLE BOOKS
5067 Ritter Road
Mechanicsburg, PA 17055
www.stackpolebooks.com

Printed in the United States of America

10 9 8 7 6 5 4 3 2 1

FIRST EDITION

Cover image from Shutterstock/Mayer George Vladimirovich
Cover design by Wendy Reynolds

Some of the sites described in this book are on private property. The authors and publisher advise readers not to trespass on private property and disclaim any responsibility for those who are prosecuted for trespassing.

Library of Congress Cataloging-in-Publication Data

Diehl, Daniel.
  Haunted houses : guide to spooky, creepy, and strange places across the USA / Daniel Diehl and Mark P. Donnelly. — 1st ed.
      p. cm.
  ISBN-13: 978-0-8117-0599-8 (pbk.)
  ISBN-10: 0-8117-0599-4 (pbk.)
  1. Haunted houses—United States—Guidebooks. 2. United States—Guidebooks. I. Donnelly, Mark, 1967- II. Title.
  BF1472.U6D54 2010
  133.10973—dc22
                                    2009046063

CONTENTS

Introduction   1

NORTHEAST

Connecticut   7
Lighthouse Inn, New London
Monte Cristo Cottage Museum, New London
Benton House Museum, Tolland
Talcott House Bed and Breakfast, Westbrook
Noah Webster House, West Hartford

Delaware   11
Woodburn, the Home of Delaware's Governor, Dover
Amstel House, New Castle
Bellevue Hall, Wilmington

District of Columbia   14
Octagon Museum, Washington
The White House, Washington

Maine   17
Kennebunk Inn, Kennebunk
Captain Fairfield Inn, Kennebunkport
Captain Lord Mansion, Kennebunkport

Maryland   20
Middleton Tavern, Annapolis
Surratt House Museum, Clinton
Schifferstadt Architectural Museum, Frederick
Hampton National Historic Site, Towson

Massachusetts   24
Porter-Phelps-Huntington Museum, Hadley
Lizzie Borden Bed and Breakfast/Museum, Fall River
Higginson Book Company, Salem
Hammond Castle Museum, Gloucester

New Hampshire   29
Mount Washington Resort, Bretton Woods
Country Tavern Restaurant and Pub, Nashua
Sise Inn, Portsmouth

New Jersey   32
Bernardsville Public Library, Bernardsville
Southern Mansion Inn, Cape May
Ringwood Manor, Ringwood
Van Wickle House, Somerset

New York   37
Belhurst Castle, Geneva
Beardslee Castle, Little Falls
Morris-Jumel Mansion, New York
Merchant's House Museum, New York
Seneca Falls Historical Society Museum, Seneca Falls
Skene Manor, Whitehall

Pennsylvania   44
Baker Mansion, Altoona
Jennie Wade House, Gettysburg
Farnsworth House Inn, Gettysburg
Harmony Inn, Harmony
Powel House, Philadelphia

Rhode Island   50
Sprague Mansion, Cranston
Castle Hill Inn and Resort, Newport
Belcourt Castle, Newport

Vermont   53
Equinox Resort, Manchester Village
Hartness House Inn, Springfield
Green Mountain Inn, Stowe
Old Stagecoach Inn Bed and Breakfast, Waterbury
White House Inn, Wilmington

SOUTHEAST

Alabama 61
The Victoria, Anniston
Gaineswood, Demopolis
Sturdivant Hall, Selma
Drish Mansion, Tuscaloosa

Arkansas 65
Peel Mansion Museum and Garden, Bentonville
Vino's Brewpub, Little Rock

Florida 67
Hernando Heritage Museum, Brooksville
The Artist House, Key West
Ernest Hemingway Home and Museum, Key West
Herlong Mansion Historic Inn and Gardens, Micanopy

Georgia 71
Warren House, Jonesboro
Hay House, Macon
Olde Pink House Restaurant, Savannah
Kehoe House, Savannah
Juliette Gordon Low Birthplace, Savannah

Kentucky 76
Liberty Hall Historic Site, Frankfort
Ashland, the Henry Clay Estate, Lexington
Loudon House, Lexington
DuPont Mansion Bed and Breakfast, Louisville
Southgate House, Newport

Louisiana 81
T'Freres Bed and Breakfast, Lafayette
Beauregard-Keyes House, New Orleans
Columns Hotel, New Orleans
Lalarie House, New Orleans
Myrtles Plantation, St. Francisville

CONTENTS

Mississippi   87
Errolton, Columbus
Cedar Grove Mansion Inn and Restaurant, Vicksburg
McRaven Tour Home, Vicksburg
Waverly Mansion, West Point

North Carolina   91
Biltmore Village Inn, Asheville
Hammock House, Beaufort
Duke Mansion, Charlotte
Mordecai House, Raleigh

Oklahoma   95
Stone Lion Inn, Guthrie
Gilcrease Museum, Tulsa

South Carolina   98
Battery Carriage House Inn, Charleston
Poogan's Porch Restaurant, Charleston
Meeting Street Inn, Charleston

Tennessee   102
Bell Witch Cave and Bell Cabin, Adams
Carnton Plantation, Franklin
Belmont Mansion, Nashville
The Hermitage, Nashville

Texas   106
Miss Molly's Hotel, Fort Worth
Ashton Villa, Galveston
Catfish Plantation Restaurant, Waxahachie

Virginia   110
Berkeley Plantation, Charles City
Kenmore Plantation, Fredericksburg
Glencoe Inn, Portsmouth
Adam Thoroughgood House, Virginia Beach
Peyton Randolph House, Williamsburg
George Wythe House, Williamsburg
Moore House, Yorktown
Nelson House, Yorktown

West Virginia   119
Federal Arsenal Guest House, Harpers Ferry
Blennerhassett Mansion, Parkersburg
Boreman Wheel House Restaurant, Parkersburg

MIDWEST

Illinois   125
Beverly Unitarian Church, Chicago
Glessner House Museum, Chicago
Culver House, Decatur
Old Slave House Museum, Junction
Voorhies Castle, Bement

Indiana   130
Old Sheriff's House and Jail, Crown Point
Hannah House, Indianapolis
Hacienda Mexican Restaurant, Mishawaka

Iowa   133
Brucemore, Cedar Rapids
Mathias Ham House, Dubuque
Villisca Ax Murder House, Villisca

Kansas   136
Tuck U Inn at Glick Mansion, Atchison
Brown Mansion, Coffeyville
Sauer Castle, Kansas City
Strawberry Hill Museum, Kansas City

Michigan   140
Felt Estate, Holland
National House Inn Bed and Breakfast, Marshall
Bowers Harbor Inn, Traverse City

Minnesota   143
Glensheen, the Historic Congdon Estate, Duluth
LeDuc Historic Estate, Hastings
Forepaugh's Restaurant, St. Paul
Gibbs Museum of Pioneer and Dakotah Life, St. Paul

CONTENTS

Missouri
148

Harry S. Truman National Historic Site, Independence
James Farm, Kearney
La Maison Guibourd-Vallé, St. Genevieve
Lemp Mansion, St. Louis

Nebraska
153

Brownville Historical Society, Brownville
Fort Sidney Museum and Post Commander's Home, Sidney
Ogallala Mansion on the Hill, Ogallala

North Dakota
156

Sage Hill Bed and Breakfast/Country Inn, Anamoose

Ohio
157

Franklin Castle Club, Cleveland
Kelton House Museum and Garden, Columbus
Buxton Inn, Granville
Chateau Laroche, the Historic Loveland Castle, Loveland
Squire's Castle, Willoughby Hills

South Dakota
164

Historic Adams House, Deadwood
Bullock Hotel, Deadwood
A Dakota Dream Bed and Breakfast, Hot Springs

Wisconsin
168

Hearthstone Historic House Museum, Appleton
Galloway House and Village, Fond du Lac
Historic 1856 Octagon House, Fond du Lac
Taliesin, Spring Green
Brumder Mansion, Milwaukee

WEST

Alaska
177

Jesse Lee Home, Seward

Arizona
178

Oliver House Bed and Breakfast, Bisbee
Riordan Mansion State Historic Park, Flagstaff

Casey Moore's Oyster House, Tempe
Buford House Bed and Breakfast, Tombstone

California   182
James Stuart Cain House, Bodie
Madrona Manor Wine Country Inn and Restaurant, Healdsburg
Stokes Restaurant and Bar, Monterey
Whaley House Museum, San Diego
Nob Hill Inn, San Francisco
Winchester Mystery House, San Jose

Colorado   188
Molly Brown House Museum, Denver
Black American West Museum, Denver
Grant-Humphreys Mansion, Denver
Rosemont Museum, Pueblo

Hawaii   192
Iolani Palace, Honolulu

Idaho   193
BJ's Bayou Restaurant, Roberts
Jameson Saloon and Inn, Wallace

Montana   196
Copper King Mansion, Butte
Hotel Meade, Bannack State Park
Brantley Mansion, Helena

Nevada   199
Bliss Mansion, Carson City
Nevada Governor's Mansion, Carson City
Metro Salon and Day Spa, Reno
Mackay Mansion, Virginia City
Gold Hill Hotel, Virginia City

New Mexico   204
St. James Hotel, Cimarron
The Lodge Resort and Spa, Cloudcroft
Old Cuchillo Bar, Cuchillo
La Posada de Santa Fe Resort and Spa, Santa Fe

CONTENTS

Oregon   208

The Chateau at the Oregon Caves, Cave Junction
McLoughlin House, Oregon City
White Eagle Saloon, Portland
Heceta Head Light Keeper's House, Yachats

Utah   213

Mary Fielding Smith House, Salt Lake City
Brigham Young Farmhouse, Salt Lake City
McCune Mansion, Salt Lake City

Washington   217

Stanwood Hotel and Saloon, Stanwood

Wyoming   218

Ferris Mansion Bed and Breakfast, Rawlins
Trail End Historic Site, Sheridan

State Index   221
Name Index   225

INTRODUCTION

Considering that sooner or later everybody is going to die,
people know surprisingly little about ghosts.

—Peter Straub

This book is designed to guide readers to the very best of America's vast array of haunted houses. In selecting the most appropriate entries for inclusion, we took many factors into consideration. First and foremost, we tried to include only houses where spiritual activity has been recorded numerous times. The second factor in our selection of sites was accessibility. Many haunted houses are not accessible to the general public, because they are either private residences or unsafe to enter. We have attempted to include only houses that are open to the public, but in a few cases, we have included exceptional houses that for one reason or another are not open. Those houses, however, are included on regularly scheduled ghost tours and contact information for the relevant tour companies has been included with the entry. Please do not approach these buildings on your own; they are private property and violators may be subject to arrest and prosecution.

As you read through the entries in this book, you will undoubtedly note that a large portion of the listings were once home to very wealthy people. This does not indicate that rich people are more likely to come back as ghosts than the rest of us. The high proportion of mansions is indicative of two simple truths: first, because of their architectural merit, mansions are more likely to survive than ordinary houses; and second, while modest haunted houses often remain as private residences, many haunted mansions have been converted to a variety of public uses.

Among the most common uses for these converted mansions are museums, restaurants, and bed-and-breakfast inns. When you visit the many commercial establishments listed in this book, please remember that they are businesses that depend on revenue for their survival and will be far more willing to answer questions about their resident ghosts if you patronize them. What could be more fun for the ghost traveler than dining or spending the night in a real haunted house?

Because we hope you will decide to visit at least a few of the many wonderful, exciting, and mysterious houses described in this book, we thought a few words on dealing with close encounters of the ghostly kind might be in order.

In your search for brushes with the otherworldly, bear in mind that ghosts, even those that appear with some degree of frequency, do not work on a schedule. Where these former members of the human race now live, time as we understand it no longer exists or operates in the same way. The unpredictability of spirit manifestations is the main reason why so many ghost-hunting television programs never capture anything more exciting than a team member claiming to have felt a touch on the shoulder. In truth, far more ghosts have been captured on film by random accident than by professional ghost hunters. You don't need tons of expensive electronic equipment to encounter a ghost. All you need is to be in the right place at the right time. Of course, even serendipity is no guarantee that you will actually see ghosts when and if they materialize. Experts in ESP (extrasensory perception) say that only about one person in ten is sensitive enough to actually see a ghost.

Assuming, however, that you are among the sensitive and happen to visit a haunted house when one of the spirits decides to manifest itself, what should you expect? As you read the entries in this book, you will discover that an uncommonly high proportion of spirits like to play with doors—slamming them shut or opening them, rattling knobs, and engaging or disengaging locks. Others appear in hallways or on staircases with almost boring predictability. According to experts in ghost behavior, this may be because doors, stairs, and hallways serve as portals between wherever ghosts usually exist and the world of the living.

Similarly, innumerable ghosts are known to interfere with battery-powered devices, such as cameras, cell phones, and pocket tape recorders, or play with electrical systems, like lights, appliances, and television sets. Some experts argue that the spirits draw minute amounts of power from electrical systems in order to maintain their temporary existence in the real world.

You will also find that ghostly manifestations fall into three main categories. One is the ghost who simply repeats movements it made while alive; these may be little more than energy echoes, spirits who are either unaware of the living or lack any degree of individual consciousness. Then there are the poltergeists, which are ghosts capable of moving objects in the physical world. Ghosts who engage in rearranging furniture or throwing objects almost never do so while they are in a visible state. We are unsure whether it is even physically possible for a visible ghost to move a solid object. Finally, there are those rare instances where a visible ghost interacts directly with the living. A few ghosts seem capable of not only appearing completely solid, but carrying on conversations and, in extremely rare instances, making physical contact with the living.

Finally, we should mention that we focus exclusively on houses in this book. There are a great many other haunted buildings in America—hotels, prisons, schools, theaters, hospitals—that can fill several volumes. For now, we are presenting the best of America's haunted houses.

Please bear in mind that all information contained in this book was correct at the time of publication. Some of the buildings, however, may have undergone changes in ownership, hours of operation, Web sites, and telephone numbers. Please contact any site you plan to visit well in advance of your arrival in order to avoid frustration or inadvertently trespassing on private property.

NORTHEAST

VERMONT

MAINE

NEW
HAMPSHIRE

MASSACHUSETTS

NEW YORK

RHODE ISLAND
CONNECTICUT

PENNSYLVANIA

NEW
JERSEY

MARYLAND

DELAWARE

CONNECTICUT

LIGHTHOUSE INN
6 Guthrie Place
New London, CT 06320
(860) 447-0299 or (877) 447-0250
www.lighthouseinn-ct.com

When steel magnate Charles Guthrie built his sprawling mansion in 1902, he named it Meadow Court. Although impressively large, the home, along with its adjoining grounds and gardens, was no more than a summer residence for the wealthy Guthrie family. But twenty-five years later Guthrie was dead; his family had divested themselves of the expense of this second mansion and Meadow Court was transformed into a very fashionable hotel and restaurant. Its name had also been changed to the Lighthouse Inn, in honor of the nearby New London Lighthouse. While such transformations typically represent a decline in the building's social standing, just the opposite was the case for the Lighthouse Inn. Attracting such Hollywood luminaries of the 1930s and '40s as Bette Davis and Joan Crawford, the Lighthouse was the "in" place to visit. It was also around this time that it started picking up the reputation of housing the ghostly entities that haunt it today.

One of the two spirits is reputed to be that of a young woman who was celebrating her wedding at the Lighthouse Inn. As she made her grand entrance down the main staircase, she tripped on her gown and fell down the stairs, breaking her neck. She died at her groom's feet. Since then her fully formed apparition has been spotted walking around the building or sitting in a corner reading, still wearing her flowing, white wedding dress. The bride has even been accommodating enough to allow a few fortunate guests to snap her picture. No one knows who the other female spirit may be, but she is frequently seen by both staff members and guests as she wanders the house in early-twentieth-century dress. There have also been reports of strange flashes of light, floating orbs, and

7

unaccountable weird noises throughout the main floor. Because of the frequency and intensity of these two ghosts—they are both fully formed and appear amazingly solid—the Lighthouse Inn occasionally holds ghost hunts and other paranormal events.

Lighthouse Inn operates as a year-round hotel and has a public restaurant serving both lunch and dinner as well as a full bar.

MONTE CRISTO COTTAGE MUSEUM
325 Pequot Avenue
New London, CT 06320
(860) 443-5378, ext. 285
www.theoneill.org/prog/monte/montprog.htm

This rambling old Victorian farmhouse was originally built in the 1840s, but it is best known as having been the boyhood home of America's only Nobel Prize–winning playwright, Eugene O'Neill, who lived here between 1900 and 1917. He later recounted his family's time in the house in his drama *Long Day's Journey into Night*. Less well-known is the fact that the house is apparently haunted by the unhappy ghost of Gene O'Neill's mother, Ella.

Ella spent much of her time here suffering from severe bouts of depression; she was probably manic-depressive, now more frequently called bipolar disorder. During more intense bouts of her illness, Ella was known to secret herself away from her family, hiding in a small room on the second floor, where she could allow her uncontrolled emotions to escape in alternate fits of weeping and laughter. Tragically, it seems that even death provided no escape for the unhappy woman. The sound of her footsteps still echoes through the little room that served as her private escape, as do the sounds of a woman crying and giggling. Visitors to the house, which is now a Eugene O'Neill museum, also report cold spots and the uncomfortable feeling of being followed.

Monte Cristo Cottage Museum is open from Memorial Day through Labor Day on Thursday through Saturday, noon to 4:00 P.M. and Sunday from 1:00 P.M. to 3:00 P.M. Groups of ten or more please call ahead. Admission fees apply.

BENTON HOUSE MUSEUM
Metcalf Road
Tolland, CT 06084
(860) 974-1875
www.tollandhistorical.org/danielbentonhomestead

Built in 1720, this wonderfully well-preserved Cape Cod–style house remained in the Benton family until 1932. Thirty-seven years later, in 1969, it was converted into a museum. During its 212 years of family occupancy, the old house saw a lot of tragedy, much of it taking place during the Revolutionary War. The house's builder and original owner, Daniel Benton, had three grandsons, and all of them were taken as prisoners of war by the British. Two died in captivity; the third, Elisha, was sent home dying of small-pox. Waiting for Elisha's return were his family and his sweetheart, Jemima Barrows. Elisha's family had refused to allow him to marry Jemima, because she was twelve years younger than he. Still the teenage Jemima volunteered to nurse Elisha on his deathbed. Elisha was buried near the driveway leading to the house, and only weeks later, the family allowed Jemima, who had also contracted the disease and perished, to be buried on the opposite side of the drive. Social custom forbid them to lay side-by-side even in death because they were not married.

Almost immediately after Jemima's burial, stories began circulating that she was seen wandering through the house, weeping pitifully, looking for Elisha. Apparently she is still trying to find him to this day. Others have reported that poor Elisha is searching for his beloved Jemima, too; the figure of a man in a Revolutionary War uniform has been seen approaching the front door, where he holds out his hands in a supplicating gesture, waits a moment, and then vanishes. Visitors to the house also hear footsteps and feel an inexplicable vibrating sensation.

Benton House Museum is open to the public on Sundays only, from June through September, 1:00 P.M. to 4:00 P.M. Admission fees apply.

TALCOTT HOUSE BED AND BREAKFAST
161 Seaside Ave
Westbrook, CT 06498
(860) 399-5020
http://talcotthouse.com

The Talcott House is one of those big, comfortable-looking Shingle-style homes from the 1890s, now operating as a bed-and-breakfast inn. No one knows why the home is haunted, and no one knows who haunts it. Nevertheless, some odd manifestations cling to the place. Guest beds un-make themselves. The old piano in the parlor plays on its own; although no one has ever seen the ghostly pianist, some people have witnessed the moving keys. Ragtime music emanates from the house's ventilation system occasionally. The spirits here are neither frequent nor particularly intense, but they have been reported many times.

Talcott House is a bed-and-breakfast that is open all year by reservation.

NOAH WEBSTER HOUSE
227 South Main Street
West Hartford, CT 06107
(860) 521-5362
www.noahwebsterhouse.org

Noah Webster's most famous book, *Webster's American Dictionary*, still occupies a firm place in many American homes and institutions. Beyond his literary and educational capacities, Webster was a tireless champion of compulsory, government-funded education and human rights. In commemoration of Webster and the American way of life in the years prior to the Revolutionary War, his birthplace, a National Historic Landmark, has been turned into a museum. Far more than a fine collection of Webster's work and memorabilia, the museum is also the home of an unidentified female spirit. Both staff and innumerable visitors have seen her shadowy figure wandering through the house's hallways carrying a lamp. Who she is, why she is here, and what she is searching for remain mysteries, but her presence has attracted enough attention that the Webster birthplace museum hosts a ghost tour every October.

Noah Webster House is open all year Thursday through Monday from 1:00 P.M. to 4:00 P.M. and is closed all major holidays and the first week of January. There is an admission fee.

DELAWARE

WOODBURN, THE HOME OF DELAWARE'S GOVERNOR
151 King Street
Dover, DE 19901
(302) 739-5656
www.woodburn.delaware.gov

Charles Hillyard III had impeccable taste and employed every bit of it when he built the stately Woodburn Mansion in 1790. So grand was this house that in 1966 it was purchased by the state for use as the governor's home. One wonders if the state was aware that old Charles Hillyard and two other permanent residents came along with the deal.

The first record of Hilliard's postmortem presence at his home dates from 1815, when a houseguest of the new owners, Dr. and Mrs. Martin Bates, passed a gentleman wearing an old-fashioned wig and knee breeches on the stairs. When he described the man to Mrs. Bates, she nearly fainted, probably because the man fit the image of her late father, Charles Hilliard. Hilliard seems particularly fond of the occasional glass of wine, and for two centuries, he has been raiding the household stock. Even Charles Terry, the first governor to live at Woodburn, from 1966 to 1969, witnessed the man in the powdered wig helping himself to a glassful from a decanter in the dining room.

Woodburn is also haunted by the ghost of a slave catcher, a bounty hunter paid to retrieve fugitive slaves prior to the Civil War. In the 1850s, Woodburn was owned by a Quaker abolitionist named Daniel Cowgill, who used the house as a stop on the Underground Railroad. On one occasion a slave catcher came to the house. Cowgill and his servants ran after the man, who then hid up an old oak tree. Entangled in the branches, the slave chaser slipped and accidentally hanged himself. The tree still stands in the yard, and the slave catcher's choking ghost is still reportedly seen dangling there.

Finally there is the little girl in the red-checked gingham dress. No one knows who she is, but since 1945 she has been seen inside and outside the house and was even spotted in the reception room during Governor Michael Castle's 1985 inauguration party. For more than two centuries, hundreds of people have witnessed the ghosts of Woodburn.

Woodburn conducts tours Monday through Friday from 8:30 A.M. to 4:00 P.M. by appointment only. It is closed on legal holidays. Admission is free.

AMSTEL HOUSE
2 East Fourth Street
New Castle, DE 19720
(302) 322-2794
www.newcastlehistory.org/houses/amstel.html

In the mid-eighteenth century, Dr. John Finney was one of New Castle's leading citizens. He counted among his friends some of the most influential people in the American colonies. Even George Washington attended a wedding at Finney's house. When the affluent Finney decided to build a residence for his son David, he sited it right across the street from his own home. The elder Finney's home, built in 1730 and now called Amstel House, was eventually rescued by preservationists and became a museum in 1929. Like his father's house, David's home is still standing across the street, and it has been converted into a restaurant. No one is quite sure why Finney connected the two houses by means of a subterranean tunnel. Even more puzzling is the identity of the ghostly presence haunting both houses and the adjoining tunnel. The most intense events take place in Amstel House, where windows open and close of their own accord and objects float through the air and out mysteriously opening doors. Despite these startling displays of levitation, no one has ever reported seeing a physical manifestation of the mysterious spirit. The Delaware Historical Society doesn't seem to mind talking about the ghost of Amstel House and every October they host a haunted tour.

Amstel House is open from April through December on Wednesday through Saturday, 11:00 A.M. to 4:00 P.M. and Sunday, 1:00 P.M. to 4:00 P.M. Admission fees apply.

BELLEVUE HALL
720 Carr Road
Wilmington, DE 19809
(302) 761-6952
www.destateparks.com/park/bellevue/index.asp

When the du Pont family emigrated from France to the United States around 1800, they did not come as penniless immigrants. As members of the old Burgundian nobility, they had stashed away a lot of cash. They immediately put it to work building an empire that has since evolved into one of the world's largest chemical companies, E. I. du Pont de Nemours, now better known as DuPont.

By the time William H. du Pont Jr. was born in 1896, he could pretty much live in any manner he pleased. He bought a grand old Gothic-style estate outside Wilmington, proceeded to transform it into an even grander estate, and named it Bellevue. In 1976, the du Pont family willed Bellevue to Delaware and with it the collection of raucous ghosts who inhabit much of the mansion's second floor and its entire third floor. No one seems to know who these restless spirits are, but their antics are so intense that the rooms they inhabit are strictly out-of-bounds for all visitors and the vast majority of the staff. Electrical appliances are routinely turned on and off, chairs move from place to place, and the sounds of laughter and screaming are reported to be so frequent that walking through the upper floors of Bellevue is like being in your own private horror movie. Curiously, no psychic research has ever been done in the house, and the management has restricted access to the affected rooms based solely on the accounts of terrified staff members, workmen, and former visitors.

Bellevue's house and grounds are open for tours during a variety of regularly scheduled events. Contact the park office or check the Web site for dates, times, and events. Private tours can be arranged for groups of ten or more by calling (302) 793-3046. Admission fees apply.

DISTRICT OF COLUMBIA

OCTAGON MUSEUM
1799 New York Avenue NW
Washington, DC 20006
(202) 626-7420
www.archfoundation.org/octagon

Col. John Tayloe III was what we today would call a mover and shaker. An entrepreneur, social gadfly, and political aspirant, Tayloe constructed between 1799 and 1801 a grand mansion near the nation's new capitol. Although the house has only six sides, it was dubbed the Octagon House. Tayloe could be a magnanimous host when it suited his political ambitions. After the British burned the White House during the War of 1812, he offered his home as temporary quarters to President James Madison and his wife Dolley. The treaty ending the war was signed on the second floor parlor.

Privately, however, Colonel Tayloe seems to have ruled his wife and fifteen children with an iron fist. One of his daughters enraged her father when she asked to marry an Englishman, and in the ensuing argument she fell down the main staircase and died. Suspiciously, and possibly tellingly, a second daughter later died during a fall down the same staircase. Hardly surprising, then, that the grand staircase has been the center point of intense spiritual activity since the mid-nineteenth century.

The Octagon House was rescued from oblivion in 1899, when it became a museum for the American Institute of Architects, and since then numerous staff and visitors have experienced the otherworldly activity around the stairs. At night, a ghostly candle is seen ascending the stairs; then a shriek is heard, followed by the sound of someone falling down the stairs. Others have heard the sound of two people walking up the stairs. Some witnesses have seen a chandelier swinging back and forth for no apparent reason and a carpet at the bottom of the stairs flinging itself back as though someone had slipped on it. Elsewhere, a female voice has been heard moaning and female footprints have been found in the dust on the attic floor. Dolley Madison's ghost is also said to have been spotted, trailing the scent of lilacs in her wake.

Octagon Museum is open all year, Monday through Friday from 8:30 A.M. to 5:00 P.M. It is closed weekends and major holidays. Entry is free to the public.

THE WHITE HOUSE
1600 Pennsylvania Avenue
Washington, DC 20500
(202) 456-7041
www.whitehouse.gov/about/tours_and_events

As a building, the White House needs no introduction, but the idea that it is haunted by at least six ghosts may come as a bit of a shock. The most famous ghost is that of Abraham Lincoln, who seemed unable to set aside his concern for his country even after his assassination in April 1865. Not surprisingly, President Lincoln's ghost is most often seen during times of national emergency and war. Several presidents and guest dignitaries have seen him. Woodrow Wilson saw him during World War I, and he appeared to Franklin D. Roosevelt and his guest, British prime minister Winston Churchill. When Queen Wilhelmina of the Netherlands was a guest, she answered a soft knocking at her bedroom door; when she opened it she found Lincoln staring down at her and promptly fainted.

During less stressful times, Lincoln was seen by Theodore Roosevelt, Harry S. Truman, and First Lady Grace Coolidge. Lincoln has been seen sitting on the bed in the Northwest Bedroom, where he quietly pulls on his boots, and he has been spotted standing in front of the oval window located above the White House's main staircase. Lincoln's son Willie, who died while his father was in office, was frequently seen during the decade following his death.

Notable ghosts of first ladies, all of whom still appear occasionally, include Abigail Adams, Dolley Madison, and Mamie Eisenhower. The most raucous spirit of all seems to be that of Andrew Jackson. Old Hickory has been known to storm up and down the second-floor hall in his high military boots, swearing like a trooper, mostly in the presence of women.

White House tours take place Tuesday through Saturday from 7:30 A.M. to 10:00 A.M. No tours are given on national holidays. Tours are free of charge, but must be arranged through your member of congress. Requests must be made at least six months in advance and are available for groups of ten or more people.

MAINE

KENNEBUNK INN
45 Main Street
Kennebunk, ME 04043
(207) 985-3351
www.thekennebunkinn.com

When a building reaches the venerable age of 180 years without experiencing any paranormal activity and then suddenly becomes haunted, the situation needs to be viewed with a critical eye and a suspicious mind. The building now known as the Kennebunk Inn was built as a private home in 1799 by Dr. Phineas Cole. It remained as a private residence until 1928, when it was converted to its present use as an inn and tavern. The building was expanded in 1940, when its name was changed to the Kennebunk Inn, and expanded again in 1980. The last expansion included the addition of six new sleeping rooms and one, or possibly two, ghosts. The disturbance caused by renovation work often stirs up restless spirits, but new construction apparently has a far more tenuous connection to the afterlife.

According to numerous sources, including the inn's own Web site, the two prime candidates for causing the spiritual activity are both former desk clerks at the inn. One of them was named Silas Perkins; he worked there during the mid-twentieth century. The other clerk is only identified by the name Cyrus and seems to have been employed at the inn only slightly earlier, during World War II. Whoever the ghostly culprit may be, both have been accused of making glasses rise from waiters' trays before crashing to the ground. Other glasses fly off the back bar and through the air. The restless, mischievous spirit (or spirits) seems to enjoy disturbing neatly arranged place settings and dragging the dining room chairs around. One guest has even reported hearing a rasping moan during a night spent at the inn.

Kennebunk Inn is a hotel and full-service restaurant and is open all year.

CAPTAIN FAIRFIELD INN
8 Pleasant Street
Kennebunkport, ME 04046
(207) 967-4454 or (800) 322-1928
www.captainfairfield.com

The Fairfields and Lords of Kennebunkport were very close. The two families were connected both professionally and socially. Several generations of Fairfield men captained ships owned by the Lords. During the first decade of the nineteenth century, Capt. James Fairfield married Lois Walker, and they received a tract of land from her father as a wedding gift. To keep the families in close physical proximity, James and Lois shared the cost of building a large double house with James's sister Polly and her husband, sea captain Joseph Lord. When the War of 1812 broke out, Fairfield and Lord went into service as privateers. Both men were captured by the British, imprisoned at London's Newgate Prison, and returned safely home to their wives in 1815. Fairfield died five years later of pneumonia at the age of thirty-six, and the following year his wife passed away also.

More than a century and a half later, the Fairfield–Lord house was converted into a bed-and-breakfast inn that was appropriately named the Captain Fairfield Inn. During the restoration process, workmen sometimes reported seeing the dark, shadowy figure of Captain Fairfield himself, hovering in the basement. A number of guests have since had similar experiences elsewhere in the house. For those asked how they knew it was really Fairfield, the answer has been that the captain's portrait still hangs in the local museum, and comparisons to the apparitions seem to verify his identity. Even those who do not actually see Captain Fairfield often insist they can sense his presence in the building.

Captain Fairfield Inn is a bed-and-breakfast that is open all through the year.

CAPTAIN LORD MANSION
6 Pleasant Street
P.O. Box 800
Kennebunkport, ME 04046
(207) 967-3141 or (800) 522-3141
www.captainlord.com

As we saw in the previous entry, both the Lords and the Fairfields were prominent, seafaring Kennebunkport families of the late-eighteenth and early-nineteenth centuries. It was the Lord family, however, that owned the ships both families sailed and, therefore, had the lion's share of the money. During the first years of the nineteenth century, the patriarch of the Lord clan was Capt. Nathaniel Lord, owner of the local shipyard. As American trade and commerce grew in the decades following independence, Nathaniel Lord prospered, but when America went to war with Great Britain for a second time in 1812, the shipping industry ground to a sudden halt. Neither desperate for cash nor wanting to lay off his shipbuilders, Lord decided to keep his men busy building his new house. The result of their effort was a grand, Federal-style mansion, with a fine spiral staircase leading up through three floors and into an enclosed cupola on the roof.

Unfortunately, Lord died before the house was finished, but his descendants continued to live in the grand old mansion for more than another century and a half, until 1972. In 1978, the house was converted into a bed-and-breakfast inn, and it was only then that reports of the ghost of Lord's widow, Phoebe, began surfacing. This is not to say the ghost was not previously present, but only that the family, if they indeed experienced her presence, never disclosed the fact. Phoebe's semitransparent specter is most often seen in the room now called the Lincoln Bedroom, where she appears in her flowing nightgown, drifting across the room and disappearing into the opposite wall. Less frequently, she is seen on the staircase leading up to the cupola. She never seems to bother the living or even give any indication that she is aware of their presence.

Captain Lord Mansion is a bed-and-breakfast inn that is open all through the year.

MARYLAND

MIDDLETON TAVERN
2 Market Space
Annapolis, MD 21401
(410) 263-3323 or (410) 269-1256
www.middletontavern.com

The building now known as the Middleton Tavern was built in 1740 for the Bennett family, but only a few years later, Elizabeth Bennett found herself a widow with no need for a large home. In 1750, she sold the house to Horatio Middleton, who operated a ferry line between Annapolis and Rock Hall, the shortest route between Philadelphia and Virginia. Because Middleton was legally required to provide overnight accommodations for his customers, he converted the Bennett home into a tavern bearing his name. As one of the few conveniently located watering holes in the area, the Middleton Tavern soon became the gathering place for the Maryland Jockey Club, the Freemasons, and an upscale social group known at the Tuesday Club. Twenty-five years after its opening, during the Revolutionary War era, the son of the late Horatio Middleton played host to such luminaries as Thomas Jefferson, Benjamin Franklin, George Washington, and James Monroe. Nearly a century later, the tavern served a short turn as a general store, but by the early 1900s, it was again a bar. At some point, the name of the tavern had changed, but in 1968, it resumed the Middleton Tavern moniker.

With such a long, colorful, and varied list of customers and owners, it is impossible to identify the ghosts that haunt the place. One entity that manifests itself visibly is in the form of a man in late-eighteenth-century clothing who stares intently out of a dining room window overlooking the Severn River. Affectionately known as Roland, this entity may be responsible for hurling plates and glasses from the shelves, overturning tables laden with dirty plates, and rearranging the chairs. Some people familiar with the building suspect this activity may be the work of prankster spirits left over from the Tuesday Club. Less identifiable are the shadowy images that occasionally move through the dining rooms.

Middleton Tavern is open for lunch, dinner, and drinks all year, Monday through Friday, 11:30 A.M. to 1:30 A.M., and Saturday and Sunday, 10:00 A.M. to 1:30 A.M.

SURRATT HOUSE MUSEUM
9110 Brandywine Road
P.O. Box 427
Clinton, MD 20735
(301) 868-1121
www.surratt.org

Pity poor Mary Surratt. In 1852, she and her husband John built a combination home, boardinghouse, and post office about fifteen miles south of Washington, D.C. The area had no name, so the postal service named it Surrattsville, after postmaster John Surratt. Despite John's drinking, life seemed stable, at least until John died in 1862, leaving Mary saddled with debt. She leased the property to a former policeman named John Lloyd and moved to the District of Columbia and into another boardinghouse she owned. Mary's son, John Jr., was an occasional tenant at both of her properties. He and his ne'er-do-well friends often met at both of the establishments. Among these companions was an actor named John Wilkes Booth, and together the group plotted the assassination of President Abraham Lincoln. During the investigation of Lincoln's murder, weapons were found stashed in John Lloyd's tavern, but it was not Lloyd who was arrested; it was Mary Surratt. Mary had not even visited the building in nearly three years. On July 7, 1865, she and three others were hanged for their alleged roles in Lincoln's murder. She was the first woman ever executed by the U.S. government. Humiliated by the scandal, the village of Surrattsville changed its name to Clinton, but the nightmare that had engulfed Mary Surratt could not be so easily expunged.

Tales of strange happenings at the former Surratt house began surfacing in the 1940s, and by the time the property became a museum in 1965, there was little doubt it was haunted. The ghostly figure of a distraught Mary Surratt is still seen moving aimlessly around the building, across the front porch and up the staircase. On the back stairs, the vague figures of men have been seen in hushed conversation and their excited voices have also been heard. Are these shadowy echoes from history, the Lincoln conspirators still plotting their horrible deed?

Surratt House Museum is open from mid-January through mid-December on Thursday and Friday, 11:00 A.M. to 3:00 P.M. and Saturday and Sunday, 12:00 P.M. to 4:00 P.M. During the months of July and August, the house is also open on Wednesday from 11:00 A.M. to 3:00 P.M. Entry fees apply.

SCHIFFERSTADT ARCHITECTURAL MUSEUM
1110 Rosemont Avenue
Frederick, MD 21701
(301) 663-3885
www.frederickcountylandmarksfoundation.org

The Brunner family immigrated to the United States from Germany in 1728. Twenty-five years later, they had saved enough money to purchase more than three hundred acres of woodland and farmland near Frederick, Maryland. In 1756, they employed the craftsmanship of their native country to build a wonderfully large stone house with walls two feet thick. They named the farm Schifferstadt, after their hometown of Scheverstadt, Germany. Over the centuries, the farm changed hands numerous times and the old house began to deteriorate. In 1972, it was slated to be demolished to make room for a gas station, but a local group of preservationists rescued and restored the house and grounds and turned them into a museum.

Apparently the renovation process awakened the spirits of the house's original owners, Joseph and Elias Brunner, and their families, because during the renovation process workers began hearing construction noises that were definitely not theirs. Electric saws and hammers make entirely different sounds than axes and mallets. Since then, the sound of ghostly feet have continued to tromp around the house and up and down the house's wooden stairs, and the sounds of voices speaking in both English and German are heard all over the building on a regular basis.

The Schifferstadt Architectural Museum is open from April 1 through mid-December, Thursday through Sunday from 12:00 P.M. to 4:00 P.M., or by special arrangements for groups. Every Friday, Schifferstadt holds a Spirit Tour of the property. Admission fees apply. While in Frederick, take in the local ghost tour held every Saturday; call (301) 668-8922 or visit www.marylandghosttours.com. Times vary according to season.

HAMPTON NATIONAL HISTORIC SITE
535 Hampton Lane
Towson, MD 21286
(410) 823-1309
www.nps.gov/hamp

It took Charles Ridgley eighteen years to complete work on his grand, Georgian-style house, but he undoubtedly thought it was worth it. With a two-and-a-half story central section capped by a fine cupola and two, single-story flanking wings, it was the largest and finest house of its type built during the early years of the nation's independence. Shortly after completing the house in 1790, Ridgley died, but the house remained in the family. Its next owner, Charles Carnan Ridgley, served as the governor of Maryland from 1815 to 1818. He probably needed such a large house, because he had eleven children and a semi invalid wife, Pricilla, who spent most of her time locked in her room severely depressed. If Pricilla Ridgley's life was unhappy, so was the death of Cygnet Swann. Cygnet was the teenage daughter of Maryland governor Thomas Swann, who was a friend of the Ridgleys. To recover from some illness, Cygnet's father sent her to stay at Hampton. Cygnet died inexplicably during her stay there.

The Ridgleys remained at Hampton until 1948. In 1979, the National Park Service took over administration of the house as a museum, but it seems that any number of the Ridgleys, their friends, and their household staff still remain in residence. Poor, sad Pricilla Ridgley appears as a fully formed entity, wearing a gray dress and cap, wandering around the house and visiting all the rooms she avoided during her long mental illness. Cygnet Swann is there, too, seated in her guest room, dressed in a satin ball gown, combing her hair. Then there is Tom, the Ridgleys' butler, who died at the end of the nineteenth century but occasionally still greets guests at the front door. On at least one occasion, this amazingly lifelike ghost reportedly escorted a guest around the entire house before vanishing. Another unknown ghost makes noises that sound like the opening of doors when no doors are moving.

Hampton National Historic Site is open from 9:00 A.M. to 4:00 P.M. seven days a week, all year long. It is closed on legal holidays. Tours are free. Groups of ten or more please call ahead.

MASSACHUSETTS

PORTER-PHELPS-HUNTINGTON MUSEUM
130 River Drive
Hadley, MA 01035
(413) 584-4699
www.pphmuseum.org

Today it seems impressive when a house remains in a family for two generations, but the old Moses Porter house remained in the same family for more than two centuries. In 1752, Porter built his fine two-story house just outside the walls of the stockade that surrounded the settlement of Hadley, Massachusetts. Sadly, only three years later, he was killed during the French and Indian War, leaving his wife Elizabeth and daughter Betty to spend the rest of their lives grieving his loss and trying to make the best of their lives. Eventually Betty remarried, and through her descendants the house remained in the family until it was turned into a museum.

Precisely when the hauntings began is unknown, because until recently the family was understandably hesitant to talk about their resident ghosts. Family tradition does tell us that odd things started happening soon after the death of Elizabeth Porter. It seems that many generations of children were sometimes tucked into bed by a glowing, ghostly presence wearing a full skirt and frilled white cap. Other reported occurrences include the whirring sound of Elizabeth's spinning wheel emanating from the attic, although the wheel has been displayed in the old kitchen for decades. The stairs leading to the attic of the original wing of the house may be the most haunted area of the building. Here, the firmly closed door opens by itself and the misty figure of an unknown, small boy has been seen running up the stairs. Elsewhere, doors have been seen to unlatch themselves, and a high-pitched musical note has been heard. In Moses and Elizabeth Porter's bedroom, visitors sometimes see the distinct impression of a body on the old four-poster bed.

Porter-Phelps-Huntington Museum is open from May 15 to October 15, Saturday through Wednesday, 1:00 P.M. to 4:30 P.M. It is open mornings by appointment only. Admission fees apply.

LIZZIE BORDEN BED AND BREAKFAST/MUSEUM
92 Second Street
Fall River, MA 02721
(508) 675-7333
www.lizzie-borden.com

According to the popular jump-rope ditty . . .

> Lizzie Borden took an ax
> And gave her mother forty whacks
> When she saw what she had done
> She gave her father forty-one

Although Lizzie may have been found innocent of the murders, popular opinion holds that she is guilty. Whatever really happened on that terrible day of August 2, 1892, it seems that Lizzie is not the only one who continues to be trapped by this long-ago crime. Now a cozy bed-and-breakfast inn, the Borden house was in a less than fashionable neighborhood when the family lived there, despite the Bordens' relatively comfortable financial position. Andrew Borden, his second wife Abby, and his two grown daughters, Lizzie and Emma, had a strained relationship, but not so bad to suggest the murders were an inside job.

More than a century after the gore-splattered corpses of Andrew and Abby were laid to their final rest, it seems that at least Abby remains on the premises. Guests and owners have reported hearing a woman weeping and the sound of footsteps going up and down the stairs and wandering around the second floor. Doors open and close and distant conversation is heard through-out the house. The most frequent phenomenon, however, is the apparition of a woman in a late-Victorian dress, presumably Abby, dusting and making the bed in the room where she was mur-dered, endlessly repeating her final actions before being struck down. In this same room, the imprint of a body occasionally appears on the bedspread and pillow, and cold spots occur here and elsewhere in the house. Electrical anomalies are common; batteries are drained in a matter of minutes and lights flicker all over the house. Outside, glowing orbs and swirling mists have been photographed on several occasions. Not surprisingly, the Borden house has been investigated numerous times.

Lizzie Borden Bed and Breakfast/Museum is open all year, and both overnight stays and tours are available. They host occasional ghost hunts and crime reenactments. You can also get a T-shirt that reads, "I Survived the Night at the Lizzie Borden Bed & Breakfast." Admission fees apply.

HIGGINSON BOOK COMPANY
148 Washington Street
Salem, MA 01970

One is forced to wonder if Joshua Ward knew what he was getting into when he built his new house back in the 1780s. Nearly a cen-tury earlier, the same site had been occupied by the home and office of Sheriff George Corwin, the man responsible for interrogating and executing those accused of "consorting with the evil one" during the nightmare farce known as the Salem Witch Trials of 1692 and 1693. There is little doubt that many of the victims cursed Corwin, along with their accusers and judges. For reasons unknown, when Sheriff Corwin died of a heart attack in 1697, his body was temporarily buried in the cellar of his house (though a possible explanation may be that he died in the winter and the ground outside was too frozen to dig a grave). Corwin was later moved, but his revenant still haunts the location of his life, death, and temporary interment, including the house Joshua Ward later built on the site.

For as long as records and legends exist, candles inside the house have inexplicably melted without the aid of a flame and objects have moved on their own. A new security system goes off on its own despite constant maintenance. People who work in the house, now home to the Higginson Book Company, have reported seeing the ghostly image of a woman roaming through the building. Cold spots are reported and the image of a woman with frizzy black hair has been photographed standing in one of the hallways. Is it possible that at least one of the nineteen people executed in the nightmare frenzy of the Salem Witch Trials really was a witch and that her dying curse still clings to the house where her executioner once lived?

Higginson Book Company is a place of business and is not open for tours, so please do not bother them.

You can see the house and other haunted buildings in the area by taking one of Salem's two ghost tours: Salem Ghost Tours, www.salemghosttours.com; Spellbound Tours, (978) 745-0138 or www.spellboundtours.com.

HAMMOND CASTLE MUSEUM
80 Hesperus Avenue
Gloucester, MA 01930
(978) 283-2080, or in winter (978) 283-7673
www.hammondcastle.org

John Hays Hammond Jr. was one of those eccentric geniuses who often appear in fiction but rarely in real life. Holding more patents than anyone in history except Thomas Edison, Hammond made a fortune from his work by the time he was nineteen and spent a fair share of it in the 1920s, when he built this magnificently creepy castle. Replete with a working drawbridge, secret passages, indoor fog and rain machines, a gigantic pipe organ, and the skull of one of Christopher Columbus' crewmen, Hammond Castle was the ideal home for a man who dabbled in spiritualism, kept a black cat for a pet, and wandered around dressed in medieval monk's robes.

Since Hammond's death in 1965, his house has become a museum and event site. It also has experienced more than its fair share of odd happenings. Items have inexplicably disappeared and reappeared, disembodied voices are heard to mutter in an unidentifiable language, and Hammond himself sometimes appears out of thin air to check on things. Hammond's wife, Irene, is also in residence and has been seen on the balcony above the organ. Furniture in the dining room has moved by itself and candelabra have been seen to rise into the air before crashing to the ground. In the Great Hall, strange shadows and lights have been seen moving along the walls. There also seems to be a very sociable, unidentified ghost, a red haired woman who has manifested herself at wedding receptions held in the castle. Hammond's strange collection of curious artifacts, the general air of medieval mystery, and the possibility of supernatural experiences makes a trip to Hammond Castle as close to visiting a real haunted castle as you are likely to get without leaving the United States.

Hammond Castle Museum is open Saturdays and Sundays only in May and the first two weeks of June, Tuesday through Sunday from mid-June through Labor Day, and Saturday and Sunday only from Labor Day to October 31. The museum is closed from Novem-

ber through the end of April. Hours are 10:00 A.M. to 4:00 P.M., but the doors close at 3:30 P.M. Group tours are available year round with two weeks advance notice. Hammond Castle also hosts occasional psychic fairs and ghost hunts, as well as special Halloween events. Check their Web site for further information. Admission fees apply.

NEW HAMPSHIRE

MOUNT WASHINGTON RESORT
Route 302
Bretton Woods, NH 03575
(877) 873-0626, (603) 278-1000, or (800) 314-1752
www.mountwashingtonresort.com

During the late nineteenth century, Joseph Stickney made a fortune in railroads and coal mining, but unlike many industrialists, he was not all work, work, work. Both he and his wife Carolyn enjoyed having people around them, loved crowds and parties, and wished they could live in the middle of a huge, unending party. So, in 1900, Joe Stickney began construction on their new house, a 314-room monstrosity of a hotel situated at the foot of Mount Washington and surrounded by 800,000 acres of national forest. Every evening, Carolyn Stickney would play hostess in the grand dining room, dressed in her jewels and finery, before retiring to a private room to dine with Joe. Sadly, in 1902, slightly less than two years after the hotel opened, Joe died of a heart attack. Carolyn stayed on at the hotel, eventually married a French prince, moved to France, was widowed again, and finally returned to the Mount Washington Hotel, where she remained until she died. Actually, that's wrong. Carolyn may have died, but there is ample evidence that she still remains at her hotel.

In Room 314 is Carolyn's favorite bed, and guests have reported seeing her sitting there, brushing her hair. Sometimes there is a knock on the door, and when it is opened, a white mist floats in. In addition to Carolyn's ghost, the Madison Room experiences the sound of a baby crying, and the rooms known as the Tower Suites have been visited by floating orbs. Electrical phenomenon here includes televisions turning themselves on and off and changing channels. In these same rooms, guests have also experienced the scent of perfume, and the bathtubs have been known to fill themselves. Throughout the hotel, the sound of ghostly music is sometimes heard and EVP has picked up disembodied voices on tape. The ever-genteel and dignified staff prefer not to discuss their ghosts.

Mount Washington Resort is open all year. Its full-service restaurant and bar are open to non-guests.

COUNTRY TAVERN RESTAURANT AND PUB
452 Amherst Street
Nashua, NH 03063
(603) 889-5871
www.countrytavern.org

The Ford House and its adjacent barn, now known as Country Tavern, was built in 1741 and owned by a Captain Ford and his wife Elizabeth. Ford captained a merchant ship and was often at sea for extended periods of time. According to both records and legend, after returning from a nearly year-long trip, Ford discovered that his twenty-two-year-old wife had given birth to a daughter. In a rage, he locked Elizabeth in a closet, murdered her daughter, and buried the tiny body near the house. When he released his wife, she attacked him and he stabbed her to death, dumping the body down the well. The fate of Ford himself is unknown.

Exactly how long after this family tragedy Elizabeth's ghost began haunting her old home is unclear, but her well-formed apparition has certainly been hanging around for nearly two centuries. In the 1980s, the Ford house and barn were converted into a restaurant and now Elizabeth has a larger audience than she could have imagined. She has manifested herself all over the house, from the dining rooms to the kitchen and even in the ladies bathroom. When fully formed, Elizabeth appears to be 5 foot, 7 inches, with ash-blond hair and wearing a white, eighteenth-century dress adorned with blue ribbons. Sometimes she remains invisible, but she still makes her presence known by moving dishes and plates, at times while people are eating from them. She moves a variety of other small objects and enjoys playing with the hair of female guests. She has also been seen staring out of one of the windows in what used to be the old barn. On rare occasions, patrons and staff have reported the disembodied sound of a baby crying. Elizabeth Ford's spectral presence has become so well known that she has made guest appearances on both *Inside Edition* and *Hard Copy*, and her story is prominently displayed on the restaurant menu.

Country Tavern Restaurant and Pub is open all year, Monday through Thursday from 4:00 P.M. to 9:00 P.M. Friday and Saturday from 4:00 P.M. to 11:00 P.M., and Sunday from 10:00 A.M. to 8:00 P.M.

SISE INN

40 Court Street
Portsmouth, NH 03801
(603) 433-1200 or (877) 747-3466
www.siseinn.com

In the vast majority of cases, houses are haunted by their former occupants—such as owners, servants, or guests—but this does not seem to be the case here. John Sise built this Queen Anne–style house in 1881 on a site formerly occupied by his wife's family home. Here, John Sise, his wife Lucy, and their daughter Mabel lived as happily as any family can reasonably expect, and eventually, the house passed to Mabel and her husband. In the 1930s, the property was sold and converted to commercial use, and between then and its reconversion into the Sise Inn in 1986, it was used as business offices, a doctor's office, a beauty parlor, apartments, and a halfway house.

At no time did anything occur that accounts for two (although some think there is only one) unusually playful ghosts recorded as living here, at least since the early 1950s. A lot of spirits seem fascinated by light switches, but the Sise Inn ghosts think larger. They operate the elevator and seem endlessly fascinated by the second-floor ice machine. On numerous occasions, when there are no guests on that floor, ice can be found scattered all along the hall and sometimes in piles melting in the guest rooms. Like many haunted houses, the doors either refuse to unlock or do so by themselves, opening and closing without human intervention. One of these entities is obviously a rather amorous male, because he is in the habit of grabbing female guests on the bottom and, on occasion, lying down on a bed next to a female patron. On one occasion a potted plant was seen to levitate and float across a room and a small rocking chair near the front desk sometimes rocks by itself.

Sise Inn is a bed-and-breakfast that is open all year.

NEW JERSEY

BERNARDSVILLE PUBLIC LIBRARY
1 Anderson Hill Road
Bernardsville, NJ 07924
(908) 776-0118
www.bernardsvillelibrary.org

Few people remember the Vealtown Tavern, which stood at this spot from 1710 onward, or the Parker family who ran the establishment during the late 1700s. But theirs is a classic ghost story. By the time Capt. John Parker bought the combination family home and inn, it was already nearly fifty years old. It had a good food and drink business, but it was small enough that Parker and his daughter Phyllis could handle it by themselves, and letting rooms brought in some extra income. One of the full-time tenants at the inn was the local physician, a young bachelor named Dr. Bryam. Nature took its course, and Phyllis and the doctor fell in love and were married.

One evening not long after the nuptials, American Revolutionary War general Anthony Wayne stopped in at the Vealtown Tavern to relax and discuss the progress of the war with a group of his officers. As the soldiers prepared to leave, Wayne discovered that some military dispatches were missing from his satchel. Several days later, a group of Wayne's soldiers returned to the tavern and arrested Dr. Bryam on charges of being a British spy named Aaron Wilde. We don't know where Phyllis was during this episode, but she was certainly there a few days later when her husband's lifeless body was returned with rope burns around his neck. According to legend, poor Phlllis went mad. Whatever happened to her, she disappeared from the historical record shortly after her husband's execution.

Eventually, Vealtown disappeared too. The old tavern became a private home, and it was in 1877, just one hundred years after the incident described above, that Phyllis began haunting her old home. The house was later incorporated into the Bernardsville Public Library and to this day Phyllis still appears near the fireplace in the reading room, looking depressed and wondering whether she really married a traitor or if her husband was wrongly executed. Occasionally, phantom footsteps are heard in the library, as are the shrieks and sobs of a woman in deep distress.

Bernardsville Public Library is open all year, Monday through Thursday from 10:00 A.M. to 9:00 P.M. and Friday and Saturday from 10:00 A.M. to 5:00 P.M. During August, Saturday hours are 10:00 A.M. to 2:00 P.M. The library is open on Sundays from 1:00 P.M. to 5:00 P.M., except in July and August, when they are closed.

SOUTHERN MANSION INN
720 Washington Street
Cape May, NJ 08204
(609) 884-7171 or (800) 381-3888
www.southernmansion.com

Industrialist George Allen wanted a summer cottage for himself and his family, so in 1863 he ordered the construction of a fine Italianate house in the up-and-coming resort town of Cape May. Surrounding the house were acres of Italian-style gardens and inside were the finest furnishings and paintings the family could find. It was a wonderful place and the Allen descendants lived there for eighty-three years. By 1946, all that remained of the family was a niece named Ester Mercur and her husband Ulysses. When Ester died, Ulysses decided to unload the old house, but it was during the middle of World War II and all he could get for the house, grounds, and furnishings was $8,000. The new owner converted the Allen estate into a boardinghouse, and by the 1980s, it had been allowed to deteriorate to the point that its license was revoked. This wonderful house stood empty until 1994, when new owners sorted through decades of garbage to rescue four tractor-trailer loads of heirlooms before completely restoring the building and opening it as the Southern Mansion Inn in 1996.

Because of the building's checkered history between 1946 and 1994, we don't know when Ester Mercur began haunting her old home, if indeed she ever left. Numerous guests and staff members have reported seeing Ester throughout the house, but she seems to have a particular fondness for the kitchen. An unusually happy ghost, she is sometimes seen dancing in the rooms and halls. Even when she remains unseen, Ester's perfume and the sound of her petticoat rustling against the walls, along with her happy laughter, alert everyone that she is still around. Guests and ghost hunters alike have taken literally hundreds of photos of glowing, floating orbs and numerous EVPs have been captured here. There are also reports of cold spots in several rooms.

Southern Mansion Inn is a bed-and-breakfast that is open all year.

RINGWOOD MANOR
Ringwood State Park
Sloatsburg Road
Ringwood, NJ 07456
(973) 962-7031 or (973) 962-2240
Group Tours: (973) 962-2241
www.ringwoodmanor.com

The grand, fifty-one room Victorian mansion now known as Ringwood Manor wasn't always quite so grand or even remotely Victorian. Like many truly old houses, it has been built, rebuilt, and remodeled numerous times over the centuries. The original portion of the house was built in 1740 by the Ogden family, who substantially enlarged it in 1762. New owners rebuilt the place from the ground up in 1807. In the 1830s, it was again massively remodeled, and even later, it was given its current Victorianized appearance by the addition of porches and abundant gingerbread decoration. Since 1932, the house and grounds have been owned by the State of New Jersey and open to the public. With all the changing ownership and reconstruction, it is hardly surprising that some residual, spiritual energy hangs around the old place.

The hauntings are both fairly subtle and only take place occasionally, so it is difficult to determine just how many ghosts actually reside here. The best guess seems to be that there are two separate spirits living at Ringwood Manor. One exists only in a small, second-floor bedroom once used by the servants, where strange sounds, footsteps, and crashing noises are occasionally heard. The other entity is thought to be responsible for opening and closing tightly locked doors and causing the creepy, clammy cold feeling that some people experience in both the first- and second-floor hallways.

Ringwood Manor is open Wednesday through Sunday all year from 10:00 A.M. to 12:00 P.M. and 1:00 P.M. to 4:00 P.M. It is closed on all national holidays except Memorial Day, the Fourth of July, and Labor Day. Ringwood advises visitors to call ahead to confirm operating hours. Admission is free, but there is a parking charge.

VAN WICKLE HOUSE
The Meadows Foundation
1289 Easton Street
Somerset, NJ 07783
(732) 828-7418
www.themeadowsfoundation.org

This charmingly simple Dutch Colonial–style house was built in 1752 by Symen and Geradina Van Wickle on land Symen's father, Evert, had given the pair as a wedding present. It seemed an ideal start in life, especially considering that Evert Van Wickle owned eight hundred adjoining acres of good, fertile farmland. Tragically, the young couple died together only five years later, when a fire swept through their new home.

The house was rebuilt, but from that time onward, the restless spirits of Symen and Geradina have inhabited the property, and along the way they have apparently picked up at least two, possibly three, companions. In 1976, the house was acquired by the local township, restored, and opened for public use, but the strange manifestations still continue. In the living room, small items have been seen to levitate in the air and hurtle themselves across the room. The door slams shut by itself, radios turn on at full volume, the door knocker on the front door knocks by itself, and dogs and cats behave very strangely, staring into space, growling, and hissing at nothing visible. In the upstairs bedrooms, people have heard their names being called along with the sound of a shrieking, screaming voice. In this same area, misty apparitions have appeared singly and in groups, and these have been captured on photos as have strange streaks of light. All over the house, small objects have been known to disappear and either turn up where they don't belong or vanish forever.

Van Wickle house is open for tours the second Sunday of every month and on numerous special events held there by the Meadows Foundation. Admission fees change depending on the event. Please call for details.

NEW YORK

BELHURST CASTLE
4069 Route 14 South
P.O. Box 609
Geneva, NY 14456
(315) 781-0201
www.belhurst.com

The history of this magnificent, chateau-style estate is certainly strange enough to have incited ghostly activities, but the identity of the ghosts of Belhurst remain mired more in legend than in fact. The first house on this idyllic site, on the shores of Lake Geneva, was built in 1826 by Joseph Fellows, who leased it out to a reclusive Englishman who called himself Henry Hall. Naming the place the Hermitage, Hall lived there alone for ten years. In 1836, after refusing to seek medical attention for a broken leg, he died of blood poisoning, and only after his death was it discovered that he had actually been William H. Bucke, former manager of London's Covent Garden Theater, who had embezzled company money, married his stepmother, and fled to New York to avoid prosecution.

Strange as that tale might be, the house's odd history continued under the ownership of Mrs. Carrie M. Y. Harron, who bought the house on a whim in 1885, tore it down, and built the fairy-tale mansion that stands there today, naming it Belhurst. Immediately upon completion of the four-year construction project, Mrs. Harron divorced her husband and married her manager.

By 1932, Belhurst had become a restaurant, speakeasy, hotel, and gambling resort operating without a license. Somehow, the new owner, Cornelius "Red" Dwyer, remained in business for a full thirty years before the federal government clamped down and forced closure of the gambling activities. Belhurst has remained a restaurant and hotel and now also operates a resort and an on-site winery, but nothing in the castle's checkered history seems to account for the supernatural activity.

Reports of hauntings date from the 1860s and 1870s, prior to the construction of the current house, and they have continued nearly uninterrupted to this day. The most famous phantom is the white-clad, female figure known to haunt the lawn of the estate, but there have been numerous glowing orbs photographed inside the castle, and hotel guests have reported having strange dreams and hearing the sounds of a crying baby and a woman singing lullabies to soothe it. Curiously, no one seems to have a viable explanation as to the origins of any of these spirits.

The Belhurst's hotel and restaurants are open all year. Wine tastings are held regularly. Please check their Web site for times and charges.

BEARDSLEE CASTLE
123 Old State Road
Little Falls, NY 13365
(315) 823-3000 or (800) 487-5861
www.beardsleecastle.com

It took three generations of Beardslees, beginning in 1790 and ending in 1860, to build Beardslee Castle, but there is evidence that the haunting began before the Beardslees even got here. During the French and Indian War, this was the site of a fortified homestead used by the local militia as an armament store. When a group of Mohawk Indians broke in, their torches ignited the gunpowder, destroyed the stores, and left some very restless Native American spirits. By 1860, Augustus Beardslee, a major stockholder in the New York Central Railroad, had completed work on the family castle, including more than a mile of imposing stone wall around the property and his own private railroad station. His son Guy lived in the house until it was gutted by fire in 1919, and the estate lay desolate until it was refurbished into a restaurant in 1944.

Shortly thereafter, motorists driving past the castle were occasionally so blinded by a ball of light whooshing across the road that numerous fatal wrecks took place. This phenomenon continues to this day. The owner of the first restaurant, A. M. "Pop" Christianson, hanged himself on the premises, and in 1989, the castle burned again despite its second floor having been closed in 1984 due to paranormal activity. Beardslee Castle is again open and fully functional, but reports of manifestations continue unabated. The most visible ghost is that of a young woman in a nineteenth-century dress, nicknamed Abigail, who wanders the grounds. Most other phenomena at the castle is less corporeal. Tables and chairs overturn on their own, silverware and glassware fly through the air, and unintelligible voices have been heard and captured on tape. Employees have been driven from the building by a shrieking voice. The sounds of footsteps and a woman singing sometimes emanate from the second floor. Doors open and close on their own and ghostly images have been captured on film. If even half of the stories about Beardslee Castle are true, this is one seriously haunted place.

Beardslee Castle is a full-service restaurant and bar with live entertainment, occasional murder mystery dinners, and Halloween events. It is open all year for dinner Thursday through Saturday from 5:00 P.M. to 8:00 P.M. and Sunday from 4:00 P.M. to 8:00 P.M. The dungeon bar remains open as late as customers remain thirsty.

MORRIS-JUMEL MANSION
65 Jumel Terrace
New York, NY 10032
(212) 923-8008
www.morrisjumel.org

In 1765, Col. Roger Morris built a lovely house in the middle of 130 acres of farmland near the northeast edge of Manhattan. Eleven years later, during the Revolutionary War, Morris and his family, staunch conservatives, fled to England, abandoning their home. In the autumn of 1776, George Washington used the empty house as his headquarters during the Battle of Long Island, and a half-dozen years later it became a tavern. Fortunately, in 1810, the house was rescued by a French wine merchant named Stephen Jumel and his conniving, manipulative American wife, Eliza. In 1832, Jumel was gravely injured when he fell on a pitchfork, but he might well have survived had his bandages not been loosened by Eliza. She escaped prosecution, but only a year later, she married seventy-eight-year-old Aaron Burr. Burr married for money. Eliza married for the dubious honor of being wife to the disgraced former vice president, who had killed Alexander Hamilton in a duel in 1804 and was arrested for treason in 1806 after plotting to establish his own country in the Louisiana Territory. They hated each other, but they both eventually died, and in 1904, their house became a museum, the last freestanding, pre-Revolution house in Manhattan.

The house is also the haunt of five known ghosts, all of whom inhabit the second and third floors. None of the spirits are seen often, but the most identifiable is Eliza Jumel Burr. Her purple-gowned figure has been seen inside the house and standing on the small balcony above the front door. Here, too, is the shade of Aaron Burr, along with the spirit of Eliza's first husband, Stephen Jumel, who remains angry over his untimely death. There is also the ghost of an unknown housemaid, who apparently committed suicide in the house, and a Revolutionary War soldier, who has been known to step out of a painting. The appearance of these ghosts is infrequent and they are not known to produce any poltergeist activity, but when they do appear they are fairly well formed and lifelike, particularly Eliza. The staff of the museum denies any ghostly activity.

The Morris-Jumel Mansion is open all year, Wednesday through Sunday from 10:00 A.M. to 4:00 P.M. and Monday and Tuesday by appointment only. It is closed on all major holidays. Admission fees apply.

MERCHANT'S HOUSE MUSEUM
29 East Fourth Street
New York, NY 10003
(212) 777-1089
http://merchantshouse.com

Gertrude Tredwell never had much of a life. Born in 1840, in her parents' fine Federal-style house in lower Manhattan, Gertrude grew up in a world where women did as they were told. In the Tredwell household, what Seabury Tredwell said was the law and not to be questioned under any circumstances. Overbearing and over-protective, Tredwell refused to give his permission for Gertrude to marry the man she loved and the denial broke both her spirit and her heart. She remained in the house, alone and reclusive, until her death in 1933 at the age of ninety-three. If posterity did anything kind for Gertrude, it was that the amazing historical value of her home, virtually unchanged since its construction in 1832, made it a perfect candidate for preservation and conversion into a museum.

Maybe the unchanging collection of family furniture, clothes, and bric-a-brac are what still draw Gertrude back like a magnet. As quiet, demure, and unassuming in death as she was in life, Gertrude's unusually well-formed specter is most often seen in the kitchen, but has also been spotted in her bedroom and other areas of the house. Even the director and employees admit the Tredwell house sometimes gives them a "cold, creepy feeling," and around Halloween they go all-out to exploit the sensation, offering a variety of reenactments including a mock nineteenth-century funeral, with tales of poor Gertrude's long, lonely life.

Merchant's House Museum is open all year, Thursday through Monday from 12:00 P.M. to 5:00 P.M. It is closed Tuesdays, Wednesdays, and all major holidays. Please make reservations for groups of ten or more. Admission fees apply.

SENECA FALLS HISTORICAL SOCIETY MUSEUM
55 Cayuga Street
Seneca Falls, NY 13148
(315) 568-8412
www.sfhistoricalsociety.org

Edward Mynderse liked his home just the way it was—a no-nonsense, mid-nineteenth-century Italianate house. But by the 1890s Mynderse was dead, and the house looked plain and outdated. The new owner gussied it up in the more modern Queen Anne style by adding towers, turrets, and verandas. Obviously unhappy at the change, Edward Mynderse made his feelings known by appearing to the living. Now more than a century after the unforgivable alterations and the house's transformation into a museum, he still pops up from time to time just to guarantee that no more ill-advised changes are made to what he still considers his home. To ensure the safety of his house, Mynderse sometimes locks the staff and guests out of certain rooms or even the entire house. He has also been known to turn pictures and paintings toward the walls and stop the clocks.

Along the way two more ghosts have taken up residence in the building, which now serves as the home of the Seneca Falls Historical Society. There is the ghost of a fifteen-year-old Irish immigrant whom the Mynderses hired as a servant, but who died of tuberculosis. Her invisible spirit pines endlessly for her faraway home on the old servants' stairs at the back of the house. The other resident ghost is a former nanny named Mary Merrigan who also died in the house and whose voice has been captured on several EVPs.

The museum is open from September through June, Monday to Friday from 9:00 A.M. to 4:00 P.M. During July and August, it is open Saturday and Sunday from 1:00 P.M. to 4:00 P.M. Tours take place on the hour. Groups over ten please call ahead for reservations. Admission fees apply.

SKENE MANOR
8 Potter Terrace
Whitehall, NY 12887
(518) 499-1906 or (518) 499-0945
www.members.tripod.com/skenemanor

Sometimes truth and legend become so entwined it is nearly impossible to sort them out. Such is the case of the ghost of the former Potter house, now known as Skene Manor. The house is a magnificent Gothic Revival mansion, built on the side of Skene Mountain in 1874 by New York State Supreme Court judge Joseph Potter. Judge Potter called his house Mountain Terrace, but the name and ownership has changed at least half-a-dozen times since Potter's death in 1902. The most significant changes took place in 1917, when then owner Dr. Ted Sachs installed a clock in the house's central tower, and in 1946, when the property became a restaurant and was renamed Skene Manor in honor of the mountain and the namesake family. The Skene story is inextricably linked with the hauntings. In the second half of the 1700s, Philip Skene and his wife settled in the area and founded a village that he immodestly named Skenesborough (now Whitehall). We no longer know where the Skene house was located; it may have been where Skene Manor now stands, but all records of its location are lost.

Legend tells us that Mrs. Skene was the one with the money, and according to her will, Philip would inherit all if she preceded him in death, but only if her body remained above ground. Not having a mausoleum handy when she died, he sealed her body in a lead coffin and placed it in the basement. Eventually he moved her out of the house and buried her in a local cemetery, but she seems to have returned to the house now named in her family's honor. By 1994, Skene Manor was abandoned and in danger of being torn down when a preservation group refurbished it and opened it to the public as a museum. At least since the 1940s, when the house was used as a restaurant, there have been reported appearances of a ghostly young woman, in late-eighteenth-century dress, wearing a striking ring on her left hand. Sometimes only her ringed left hand appears. At other times, she materializes fully formed for a few seconds before turning into a glowing orb.

Skene Manor is open April through October, Wednesday to Sunday from 11:00 A.M. to 4:00 P.M. From November through March, please phone for special group tours. During the regular season, the tea room is open for lunch Friday through Sunday. Tours are free.

PENNSYLVANIA

BAKER MANSION
Blair County Historical Society
3419 Oak Lane
Altoona, PA 16602
(814) 942-3916
www.blairhistory.org

Like many successful businessmen, Elias Baker was a thrifty, hard-working tyrant. He hated the fact that he needed his cousin's help to go into the iron-smelting business in 1836 and bought his cousin's share as quickly as possible. Ruling his wife and family with the same iron fist he used on his workers, he made every decision. The construction of his new mansion, however, nearly proved more than even Baker could handle. Beginning in 1845, a series of minor disasters, cost overruns, and collapsing iron prices meant that the house would not be completed until 1849, and by that time Baker was nearly bankrupt. Taking his financial frustrations out on his family, Baker decided their every move. When daughter Anna asked permission to marry the man she loved, Baker refused, because the man was a simple ironworker. By the time Baker died in 1864, his family was as miserable as he had been. His widow lived for thirty-five more years, but she never remarried, and two of his four children never married at all, remaining in the house until they died.

When Anna, the last of the Bakers, died in 1914, the house became a museum, but the bitterness and cruelty that had poisoned Baker life continued to linger, along with at least three unhappy spirits. The old dining room is notable for occasional cold spots, floating orbs, and the specter of Elias Baker himself. Normally fearless K-9 dogs, called in to investigate a reported break-in, refused to enter the dining room. In the basement ice room, where the body of son David was kept through the winter of 1852 after an accidental death, occasional screams have been heard. Ghostly faces have been seen in mirrors throughout the house. There is also a female figure dressed in black who moves up and down the stairs to the third floor. The most frequent and famous haunting, however, is the wedding dress in Anna Baker's bedroom; it moves and flutters inside its locked glass case. The dress was not Anna's, of course, so most people believe she is violently shaking a mocking symbol of the wedding she was never allowed to have.

Baker Mansion is open June through August, from Tuesday to Friday, 1:00 P.M. to 3:00 P.M., and Saturday from 12:30 P.M. to 2:15 P.M. It is closed Sunday and Monday. The remainder of the year, the mansion is open by appointment only. Admission fees apply.

JENNIE WADE HOUSE
528 Baltimore Street
Gettysburg, PA 17325
(717) 334-4100
www.gettysburgbattlefieldtours.com/jennie-wade-house.php

The Battle of Gettysburg was a bloody, three-day affair that took the lives of nearly 8,000 men and left 25,000 severely wounded. Considering the degree of carnage, it is a miracle that only one civilian was killed. When the battle opened on July 1, 1863, Confederate forces drove back the Union troops, capturing much of the town in the process. As civilians fled, twenty-year-old Mary Virginia Wade, known as Ginnie, hurried to the home of her sister, Georgina McClellan, on Baltimore Street. With a four-day-old infant, Georgina refused to leave and Ginnie insisted on staying to help her. Despite being trapped in a no-man's-land between Union and Confederate snipers and artillery emplacements, suffering through more than 150 bullets and a ten-pound artillery shell slamming into the house and breaking every window, the two women tended the baby and passed out food and water to the Union troops. At 8:30 A.M., on July 3, the final day of the battle, Ginnie was in the kitchen making bread when a minié ball crashed through two doors and struck her in the back, piercing her heart. The newspaper account of her death misspelled Ginnie's name, erroneously calling her Jennie, the name that would go down in history. The bullet holes were never repaired, and the house became the first museum dedicated to the Battle of Gettysburg, remaining much as it was at the time, including the presence of Ginnie Wade.

Visitors claim to smell fresh-baked bread in the kitchen and dozens of floating orbs have been photographed in nearly every room of the house. On the opposite side of this double house, which suffered nearly as much damage as the McClellan home, the figure of a woman in Civil War–era clothing has been photographed in a second floor bedroom mirror. There is also evidence that a second ghost resides here, that of the Wade girl's father, who is said to account for at least some of the spirit orbs, particularly in the basement where his daughter's body was kept for two days until it was safe to remove her for burial. Many of the eerie photos described above can be viewed in a basement display and in a photo album kept in the gift shop.

Jennie Wade House is open April through September from 9:00 A.M. to 7:00 P.M., seven days a week. During October, November, and March, hours are from 9:00 A.M. to 5:00 P.M., seven days a week. The house is closed December through February. Admission fees apply.

FARNSWORTH HOUSE INN
401 Baltimore Street
Gettysburg, PA 17325
(717) 334-8838
www.farnsworthhouseinn.com

The horror of battle frequently leaves specters lingering at the place of their death and nowhere is this truer than in Gettysburg. The three-day Civil War battle fought there in July 1863 left more men dead in a shorter period of time than the D-Day invasion of Normandy during World War II. Inevitably the battle spilled over into the town, and among the buildings occupied was the home of the Sweeny family. Confederate sharpshooters stationed in the attic picked off Union soldiers and one innocent civilian, twenty-year-old Jennie Wade.

For well over a century the Sweeny house, now the Farnsworth House Inn, has been known to be haunted. Confederate soldiers still tramp around the attic, dragging boxes and trunks to use as breastworks. A former local midwife and nurse named Mary still tends to the living, thinking they are ill or wounded, and a small boy who was run down by a wagon and brought to the house to die still lingers here. In all, there are at least fourteen ghosts in the house, making it the seventh most haunted house in the nation.

Those who spend the night in the Shultz Room or the Sara Black Room often feel, and sometimes see, Mary sitting on the corner of their bed. Sometimes they have their covers tucked tightly around their neck while Mary whispers, "You have to sweat out the fever." Door knobs shake violently, the specters of horribly wounded soldiers stalk the halls, and ghostly blood has been seen to run down the walls of the second-floor bathroom, presumably coming from wounded soldiers in the attic. Unused beds become wrinkled, their pillows showing the indentation of a head. The smell of cigar smoke comes from nowhere, and numerous recordings of disembodied voices called EVP have been taken. A 1999 photo of Mary's ghost, hovering over a bed, hangs in the lobby. Of the nine guest rooms at the Farnsworth House, five are reportedly haunted.

Farnsworth House Inn is open all year. There is a full-service restaurant and bar open to the public for lunch and dinner from 11:30 A.M. daily. The inn also offers numerous special events, such as magic shows, ghost stories, a séance, and a recreated Victorian funeral parlor. Live entertainment takes place Friday and Saturday, May through November. They also host the Gettysburg Ghost Walk; see www.gettysburghauntedaddress.com.

HARMONY INN
230 Mercer Street
Harmony, PA 16037
(724) 452-5124
www.historicharmonyinn.com

The Harmony Society was a communal sect of German Protestant pacifists who came to America in the early nineteenth century. The Harmonists settled in western Pennsylvania in 1804, but ten years later had outgrown their town so they sold the village to a Mennonite group and moved to Indiana. The Mennonites remained in Harmony, but many non-Mennonites moved there. In 1856, a local banker, mill owner, and railroad speculator named Austin Pearce built a fine Italianate house here. Unfortunately, Pearce's railroad speculations were less than profitable and within twenty years, his house had been sold and converted into a hotel. Over the years, the building, now known as the Harmony Inn, has changed hands at least six times and been used as a private home, a livery stable, a boardinghouse, and a restaurant. With this long and rich history, it is small wonder that the building has collected at least four ghosts.

In the attic lives the shade of an elderly woman in a long black dress who materializes and vanishes in front of startled visitors. There are also the ghosts of a small boy whose photo hangs in the building and a teenage girl with a pronounced limp who has been seen in the restaurant area. The final ghost is that of a man known only as Barney, who is blamed for moving small objects and later returning them. Visitors have reported having things removed from their pockets and experienced unexplained cold spots and air currents. Furniture has been moved unaided by living hands and the image of a male face has appeared in mirrors. It is worth mentioning that the entire town of Harmony is now a National Historic District and much of it is reportedly haunted. There have been sightings of a World War II–era pilot walking the streets and a lumberjack carrying an ax in a private home. At the Harmony Inn, a raft of media coverage is proudly displayed in the bar area.

Harmony Inn is open for lunch and dinner seven days a week all year. There is live music on the front porch several times a month during the summer. The inn is closed on Christmas day.

POWEL HOUSE
244 South 3rd Street
Philadelphia, PA 19106
(215) 627- 0364 or (215) 925-2251
www.philalandmarks.org/powel.aspx

Charles Stedman had no intention of selling his grand house on what was known in the late eighteenth century as Philadelphia's "Millionaires Row," but when faced with the choice to sell or be hauled off to debtors prison, the three-year-old house went to Samuel Powel in 1769. Powel was a mover and shaker in late colonial Philadelphia; he was both the city's last mayor under British rule and its first under American rule, as well as a friend of George Washington, the Marquis de Lafayette, and many signers of the Declaration of Independence, all of whom he entertained in his home.

By 1900, the once prosperous neighborhood had come down in the world, and Powel's house was reduced to use as a warehouse. The owner stripped out and sold nearly all of the interior decoration and woodwork, and by 1930, the house was little more than a shell and was slated for demolition. Fortunately, the city's first preservation group was formed specifically to save the Powel House, and by the time World War II rolled around, the grand house was virtually indistinguishable from its original appearance. As often happens, the process of bringing the house back to life also brought back a collection of spirits. General Lafayette frequently returns from his grave in far-off France, accompanied by a group of colonial militiamen, and together they enter the house through the closed front door. On the second floor is the breathtakingly lifelike ghost of a young woman in a beige and lavender eighteenth-century ballgown who fans herself, smiles demurely, and nods at visitors before slowly dematerializing. For unknown reasons, the ghost of the duplicitous Benedict Arnold has also been sighted in the house. Maybe he is still doing penance for attempting to betray his country.

Powel House is open all year on Thursday, Friday, and Saturday from 12:00 P.M. to 4:00 P.M. and Sunday from 1:00 P.M. to 4:00 P.M. Saturday tours may be limited because of special events. Advance reservations are required for groups of ten or more.

RHODE ISLAND

SPRAGUE MANSION
Cranston Historical Society
1351 Cranston Street
Cranston, RI 02920
(401) 944-9226
www.cranstonhistoricalsociety.org

Cranston was once so dominated by the Sprague family that the town's original name was Spragueville. William Sprague built his farmhouse in 1790, but his fortune began eighteen years later when he built a textile printing mill where he churned out miles of inexpensive printed cotton fabric known as calico. The fabric made his family one of the most powerful names in Rhode Island. The burgeoning Sprague empire passed to William's sons, Amasa and William, and while William went into politics, Amasa tended the business and enlarged his house into the mansion it is today. But with money comes enemies. On December 31, 1843, Amasa left home for a business trip, but the following day his battered corpse was found near the edge of the family estate. Despite the lack of witnesses and evidence, the entire family of a local tavern owner, Nicholas Gordon, was arrested and charged with conspiracy to commit murder. Nicholas' brother, John, was found guilty and hanged, but new evidence later proved he was innocent.

Kate Chase Sprague, William's widow, became the first reported entity to haunt the Sprague mansion when she was sighted in 1925, twenty-six years after her death. By the time the Cranston Historical Society acquired the mansion in 1966, both she and Amasa, who is seen walking down the main staircase, were making occasional appearances. Only a year later, a group of live-in caretakers made contact with another ghost via Ouija board. This spirit called himself Charlie and said he had been a butler for the Sprague family. A variety of phenomena, such as cold spots, disembodied voices, and a "filmy white thing" all manifest themselves. But it is Charlie who has become the star of the Sprague mansion's non-living cast. He plays host to their annual Halloween party, although he has never shown up, and those interested in finding out more about ghostly goings-on at the Sprague mansion can contact him by email at charliethebutler@verizon.net.

Cranston Historical Society's Sprague Mansion is available for private functions and is open for tours by appointment. They also host annual Halloween parties. Admission fees apply.

CASTLE HILL INN AND RESORT
590 Ocean Drive
Newport, RI 02840
(401) 849-3800 or (888) 466-1355
www.castlehillinn.com

The wonderfully sprawling Victorian mansion now known as the Castle Hill Inn, perched on the shores of the Atlantic Ocean, was once the summer home and research center of Alexander Agassiz. Agassiz's fascination with sealife laid the foundation for the modern science of marine biology. Agassiz went so far in promoting the study of sealife that he founded Harvard's Museum of Comparative Biology and endowed it with more than a million and a half dollars, an impressive amount of money at the close of the nineteenth century. When Agassiz died in 1910 his house passed into the hands of his son and daughter-in-law, but following a massive flood in 1938, they sold the property. It has since been transformed into an upscale inn and restaurant.

Precisely who the female spirit is that haunts the inn is unknown, but she is assumed to be the late wife of one of the facility's former managers. She has only appeared on a few occasions and only to members of staff, but she regularly makes her presence known by randomly and sometimes violently rearranging the dishes in the pantry.

Castle Hill Inn and Resort is open all year. In addition to nine guest rooms, it has four dining rooms that are open to guests and the general public for lunch, dinner, and Sunday brunch. Reservations are recommended. Dress code is business casual.

BELCOURT CASTLE
657 Bellevue Avenue
Newport, RI 02840
(401) 846-0669
www.belcourtcastle.com

Oliver Hazard Perry Belmont hated his neighbors. When he built this fabulous French Chateau–style estate between 1891 and 1894, he situated it so the neighbors were forced to look at the back of the building. This would seem like insult enough, but the $3 million, sixty-room mansion had only one bedroom, one bath, and no kitchen. The entire ground floor was used to stable the horses, but since it was only intended as a summer cottage, none of this mattered. Belmont and his wife, Alva, spent most of their time traveling the world, collecting art and antiques, and cramming them into Belcourt. Oliver Belmont died in 1908 and his wife followed in 1933. Seven years later, the estate was sold and began a long slide into disrepair. In 1956, the Tinney family bought and restored Belcourt, and although it is a private residence, the house along with its fabulous collection of antiquities is open to the public.

Unlike the other properties listed in this book, Belcourt itself does not seem to be haunted. The hauntings instead emanate from some of the objects in Belmont's vast collection of antiques. In the magnificently creepy Gothic Ballroom, adorned with old tapestries, paintings, and sculpture, guests will find a suit of armor whose original owner died when a lance pierced his visor.

Since then the unfortunate knight is heard to scream during the month of March, when his death occurred. Also in the ballroom is a pair of haunted chairs, one of which has been known to forcibly eject people. There is a statue of a monk that holds the monk's ghost; he also occasionally appears and roams the rooms and halls, walking through walls at will. The most stomach-churning object in the house, however, is a mirror that refuses to reflect the image of people standing right in front of it, showing only moving images that shift back and forth. Belcourt's collection may contain the most haunted objects in the world, and they seem to display their paranormal powers on an almost constant basis.

Belcourt Castle is open throughout the year on Wednesday through Monday from 12:00 P.M. to 5:00 P.M. Candlelight tours are held Friday through Monday at 6:00 P.M. and 7:00 P.M. Ghost tours are available April through November on Thursday and Saturday at 5:00 P.M. and all of Halloween week. Advance reservations are suggested. Fees are charged for all tours.

VERMONT

EQUINOX RESORT
3567 Main Street
Manchester Village, VT 05254
(802) 362-4700
www.equinoxresort.com

When William Marsh opened his tavern in Manchester in 1769, it amounted to nothing more than two large rooms on the main floor and family living quarters on the second floor. With little competition in the area, Marsh attracted Revolutionary War–era luminaries Ethan Allen and his brother Ira, founders and leaders of the Green Mountain Boys militia. Here, the Allens planned to confiscate the property of colonists loyal to Britain, and they started with Marsh Tavern. Over the ensuing years, the tavern changed hands many times. In 1853, it was combined with the nearby home of L. C. Orvis, expanded to a whopping two hundred rooms, and renamed Equinox House. During the summer of 1862, First Lady Mary Todd Lincoln, who was mourning the recent loss of her eleven-year-old son Willie, came here with her surviving sons Robert and Tad in order to escape the heat and humidity of Washington. Two years later Mrs. Lincoln and the boys returned, and the entire Lincoln family had planned to make a return visit in 1865. But by then the president had been murdered, and the distraught Mrs. Lincoln did not return.

Since then, through many expansions, renovations, and the fifteen years during the 1970s and early 1980s when the Equinox stood abandoned and boarded up, Mary Lincoln has often returned to the Equinox, where she and Willie wander the third-floor hallways, appearing and quickly vanishing before startled guests and staff. Sometimes they appear as fairly well-formed entities, and at other times, they simply rumple up freshly made beds. Staff and guests have reported hearing whispered, disembodied voices and finding small items moving from their appointed places. Equinox has been investigated several times by reputable paranormal investigators and all confirm the presence of ghostly activity, although they have not positively identified Mary Lincoln.

Equinox Resort is open all year. In addition to hotel and dining facilities open to the public, the resort offers golf, skiing, special events, and even a falconry school.

HARTNESS HOUSE INN
30 Orchard Street
Springfield, VT 05156
(802) 885-2115 or (800) 732-4789
www.hartnesshouse.com

James Hartness was one of those rare individuals referred to as a renaissance man. A businessman and inventor, Hartness ran the Jones & Lamson Machine Tool Company, beginning in 1889. By then he had already begun churning out a string of inventions, which by the time he retired in 1933 brought him income from 120 patents. In addition to being an engineering whiz, Hartness was an amateur aviator and friend of Charles Lindbergh. He served as governor of Vermont from 1921 to 1923, and in his spare time, he was an avid astronomer. To further his astronomical pursuits, he built a large telescope on the front lawn of his 1904 house. For privacy, he constructed a series of underground rooms, offices, and shops beneath the lawn and telescope.

When the Hartness house was converted for use as a country inn, the telescope and subterranean workshops were allowed to remain and both can be seen by the public. It is in James Hartness's secret world that the reports of ghostly activity seem to have originated. Guests to the subterranean rooms have the slightly uneasy feeling that someone is constantly watching them. Both here and in the main inn, the electricity is known to go out for periods of more than an hour with absolutely no technical explanation. Visitors also report small objects inexplicably moving from place to place or disappearing entirely.

Hartness House Inn is open all year. They offer both bed-and-breakfast and hotel accommodations, along with a restaurant and bar that are open to the public.

GREEN MOUNTAIN INN
18 Main Street
Stowe, VT 05672
(802) 253-7301 or (800) 253-7302
www.greenmountaininn.com

Peter Lovejoy's maid fell in love with his groom, and the two were wed. The story of two servants marrying is hardly spectacular, but when Lovejoy sold his seventeen-year-old house in 1850, it was converted into an inn and the servants remained in residence to work for the new owner. By this time, the couple in question, the Berrys, had a ten-year-old son, who in the early 1860s inherited his father's job as groom to the hotel's horses.

Alcohol eventually got the better of the young lad, and he lost his job, drifted around the country between spells in local jails, and eventually found his way back to Stowe in January 1902. The only thing he had learned during his thirty-year absence was how to tap dance, earning him the nickname Boots Berry. When he found out his birthplace was now a hotel owned by Mark Lovejoy, Peter's son, Boots dropped in, hoping to find a warm bed and a hot meal. Mark Lovejoy was a charitable man, so he took Boots in and gave him a room. Only days after Boots returned, a nightmarish blizzard descended on the town. Somehow, a small girl, whose parents were guests of the hotel, crawled out onto the roof; she was in imminent danger of freezing or being swept off by the gale. Boots quickly remembered an old access passage to the roof. Climbing onto the ice-and-snow-covered shingles, he helped the little girl to safety, but before he could return inside, he slipped and fell to the ground, breaking his neck.

Boots is still there at the hotel, although it has undergone several incarnations and a massive restoration project in the more than one hundred years since his death in 1902. On winter nights only, staff and customers swear they can hear him tap dancing up on the third floor in Room 302, where he was born, just a few feet above the spot where he fell to his death sixty-two years later.

Green Mountain Inn is open all year. It offers hotel accommodations, apartments, and a full-service restaurant and bar open to the public.

OLD STAGECOACH INN BED AND BREAKFAST
18 N. Main Street
Waterbury, VT 05676
(802) 244-5056 or (800) 262-2206
www.oldstagecoach.com

The precise origins of the house now known as the Old Stagecoach Inn are nearly lost in the maze of history. We know the three-story, Federal-style building was constructed in 1826 for use as both a home and an inn, but records conflict as to whether the original owner was either a man named Parmalee or Daniel Carpenter, Waterbury's first lawyer. There is even more confusion over who actually built the structure. Curiously, at some point during the middle of the nineteenth century, the house and nearby barn were both painted black; they had been returned to a more normal white by 1880, when listed as the summer home of a Miss Annette Henry. By that time, however, Annette was no longer Miss Henry but Mrs. Albert Spencer. Her husband had made a fortune in Ohio in Akron's burgeoning rubber industry, and within a few years of their marriage, the couple owned a suite at New York's Waldorf Astoria; a house in Newport, Rhode Island; and apartments in Paris and London. In a move that did not make Annette any more popular in her hometown than did her vast wealth or scandalous habits of smoking cigarettes and chewing tobacco, she had the Federal façade of the Waterbury house overlaid with elaborate Victorian-style porches. When Albert Spencer died of an undiagnosed illness in London in 1907, local gossip naturally pointed an accusing finger at his widow. Domineering, opinionated, and rich enough to do as she pleased, Annette moved back to Waterbury and spent her remaining years infuriating her neighbors.

After Annette's death in 1947, the house went through several owners; it was alternately renovated and abandoned until it was transformed into the Old Stagecoach Inn Bed and Breakfast in 1993. Only then were the decades-old stories of odd occurrences in the house confirmed. An old woman in a white shawl appears in the rocking chair in Room 2, Annette's old bedroom. Pieces of furniture move on their own and freshly made beds are found stripped bare, the blankets neatly folded and stacked at the foot of the bed.

Old Stagecoach Inn Bed and Breakfast is open all year.

WHITE HOUSE INN
Route 9
P.O. Box 757
Wilmington, VT 05363
(802) 464-2135 or (800) 541-2135
www.whitehouseinn.com

Martin Brown was a lumber baron who made his fortune from Vermont's vast tracts of timber, so when he decided to build a new house in 1915, both the cost and the amount of lumber involved was completely irrelevant. The resulting thirty-room house looked more like an antebellum plantation mansion than something in conservative New England; so it was hardly surprising when the Brown house was eventually transformed into a hotel and renamed the White House.

That the Browns loved their home and hated to leave even in death is evidenced by the late Mrs. Brown's return to the house soon after her demise. Both guests and staff have reported unexplained cold spots, doors slamming open and closed, and spectral presences for decades. Sometimes the late Mrs. Brown is barely visible, appearing as little more than a mist, and at other times she is clearly visible and nearly solid. According to the White House's management, on one occasion, when a woman whose name happened to be Mrs. Brown was staying at the hotel, the resident ghost appeared next to the sleeping woman's bed and in a stern voice said, "One Mrs. Brown in this room is quite enough." Having made her feelings known, the late Mrs. Brown then promptly vanished. White House Inn seems rather proud of their resident spirit, and every Halloween they host a ghost hunt and séance.

White House Inn is open all year. Its full-service restaurant is open to the public.

SOUTHEAST

WEST
VIRGINIA

VIRGINIA

KENTUCKY

NORTH
CAROLINA

TENNESSEE

OKLAHOMA

ARKANSAS

SOUTH
CAROLINA

GEORGIA

ALABAMA

TEXAS

LOUISIANA

MISSISSIPPI

FLORIDA

ALABAMA

THE VICTORIA
1600 Quintard Avenue
Anniston, AL 36202
(256) 236-0503
www.thevictoria.com

Like a lot of oversized old mansions that have outlived their useful-
ness as private homes, the Queen Anne-style Victoria mansion,
built in the 1890s, has been converted into a hotel and restaurant.
Nobody seems to know who the ghost at the Victoria is, but from
occasional appearances on the upstairs landing, it is obvious that
it's a female. Seemingly right at home among the guests and staff,
her footsteps can be heard throughout the hotel, and she can
sometimes be heard clinking invisible glasses behind the bar. Most
spectacularly, she makes an occasional guest appearance in the
piano lounge, where guests and staff have heard and seen her
playing the piano. She has never been known to bother anyone,
but appears to be quite happy in her surroundings. The feeling is
returned by those who have experienced her.

*The Victoria's hotel and restaurant are open all year. For hotel
reservations only, call (800) 260-8781.*

GAINESWOOD
805 South Cedar
Demopolis, AL 36732
(334) 289-4846
www.preserveala.org/gaineswood.aspx

What is now the magnificent Gaineswood plantation museum
started out as nothing more than George Gaines's two-room
cabin, built back in 1821. Then in 1843, Gaines sold his cabin
and 480 acres to a cotton planter named Nathan Whitfield, who

between 1844 and 1861 built the astounding 6,215-square-foot Greek Revival mansion we see today. Sadly, Whitfield's wife Betsy died in 1846, so he employed the services of a refined young Virginia lady named Evelyn Carter to raise his children and act as hostess to his guests. Evelyn was a fine nanny and talented singer and musician, but several years after her arrival at Gaineswood, she fell ill and died. Her final request was that her body be returned to her family plot in Virginia, but for whatever reason, her dying wish was never fulfilled.

Trapped eternally at Gaineswood, Evelyn seems determined to make the best of her situation. In addition to the sounds of her hoop skirts rustling against the walls, whispered voices, and delicate footsteps going up and down the long staircase, Evelyn began giving piano and vocal recitals when the house's original piano was returned (along with many other original furnishings) during Gaineswood's restoration in the 1970s. This is particularly astonishing, because the piano, built during the 1840s, has not worked in decades. In addition to Evelyn, it seems that either old George Gaines or Nathan Whitfield comes back now and again; the smell of a man's pipe is often detected in the study. Gaineswood's staff is more than happy to discuss Evelyn with guests.

Gaineswood is open Tuesday through Friday from 9:00 A.M. to 4:00 P.M. The museum is open by appointment on weekends and Mondays for groups of ten or more. It is closed on legal holidays. Admission fees apply; children under age six are free. Tours take one hour.

STURDIVANT HALL
713 Mabry Street
Selma, AL 36701
(334) 872-5626
www.sturdivanthall.com

Although the Civil War raged all around him, John Parkman's life seemed pretty good. In 1864, at the age of twenty-six, he was president of the First National Bank of Selma. and he bought an eleven-year-old mansion in the center of town for himself and his family.

When the South lost the war, however, things quickly went very, very bad. While Selma was occupied by Union troops, Parkman was arrested on possibly trumped-up charges of embezzling bank funds and thrown into federal prison, where he died during an alleged escape attempt in 1867 at the age of twenty-nine. To this day, questions remain as to whether he actually tried to break out or was murdered and the escape attempt was a story concocted to conceal the crime. In either case, Parkman was dead and his wife was left without support for herself and her two daughters. In 1870, Sarah was forced to sell the mansion for one-fifth of its appraised value.

When the new owners took possession of Sturdivant Hall, however, it seems that John Parkman was there to meet them. From that day to this, Parkman's ghost has been seen on the side porch and in the cupola on the roof, and his footsteps have been heard wandering around the second floor hall toward the bedrooms. At night, the shutters, which are always locked and cannot be opened without unlocking the windows, are inevitably standing open, and the back door of the house unlocks, opens, and closes on its own. Additionally, the ghostly figures of two small girls, presumably Parkman's daughters, have been seen peering out of the second floor windows. A servant's house at the rear of Sturdivant Hall is also haunted by a spirit who insists on rearranging pictures and other small objects on display. Sturdivant Hall has been a museum since 1957.

Sturdivant Hall is open Tuesday through Saturday from 10:00 A.M. to 4:00 P.M. An admission fee is charged.

DRISH MANSION
2300 17th Street
Tuscaloosa, AL 35401

When Dr. John Drish married Sarah McKinney in 1835, they were both relatively young, widowed, and rich enough to indulge their tastes. In 1837, they began building a fine Italianate/Greek Revival mansion in the center of a 350-acre plantation on the outskirts of Tuscaloosa. During the 1860s, they added an impressive three-story tower on the front of the house. The couple had two daughters, and life should have been good at the Drish home, but John developed a gambling problem and tried to wash away the pain of his huge losses with ever-increasing amounts of booze. By the time his children were grown, he had become an insufferable tyrant, and when his eldest daughter Katherine fell in love, Drish adamantly refused to let her marry, going so far as to buy off her suitor. Katherine slowly went insane with grief.

Still, Sarah loved her husband, and when he died as a result of a fall during a bout of delirium tremens, she filled the house with candles during his wake. Later, Sarah insisted the same candles be used at her own funeral, but when the time came the candles could not be found. Only months later, a brigade was called to extinguish a fire in the tower, but when they got there, there was no fire. This same scenario has been carried out numerous times over the years, and the spirit of John Drish is said to be heard screaming and falling down the same staircase that caused his death. It seems that daughter Katherine is also there, entering the rooms of overnight guests, touching their cheeks, and pulling up their covers. The Drish mansion was abandoned, but it recently has been acquired by a local preservation group who are restoring the house and plan to open it to the public.

Drish Mansion is currently closed to the public and is unsafe to enter. Trespassers will be prosecuted. To check on the progress of the restoration, call the Tuscaloosa County Preservation Society at (205) 758-2238.

ARKANSAS

PEEL MANSION MUSEUM AND GARDEN
400 S. Walton Boulevard
Bentonville, AR 72712
(479) 273-9664
www.peelmansion.org

In 1875, former Confederate colonel Samuel Peel built a splendid Italianate villa for his family on the outskirts on Bentonville. Replete with towers and turrets, the fine brick house stood at the center of a working farm that included elaborate formal gardens and more than 180 acres of apple orchards. Peel and his wife, Emaline, raised their nine children in the grand old house. Peel then went on to become Arkansas's first native-born member of the U.S. House of Representatives. Today the Peel Mansion is a museum that features a stunningly recreated nineteenth-century interior complete with period lighting fixtures.

The ghosts at the Peel Mansion are anonymous. Numerous staff members and guests have reported seeing strange moving shadows from the corners of their eyes, but when they turn to look at them, the apparitions disappear. Staff have also witnessed both small and large objects moving from place to place with a fairly regular degree of frequency.

Peel Mansion Museum and Garden is open all year, Tuesday through Saturday from 10:00 A.M. to 4:00 P.M. During the last week of October the site sponsors a ghost walk that begins at the mansion. In early December, they host a holiday open house. Check their Web site for specific dates and times of the special events. Admission fees apply.

VINO'S BREWPUB
923 West 7th Street
Little Rock, AR 72201
(501) 375-8466
www.vinosbrewpub.com

Like many late-nineteenth-century buildings, the old commercial structure that now houses Vino's Brewpub was originally designed to have a business on the ground floor and domestic quarters for the owner and his family on the floor above. Records concerning much of the building's past are lost, so there is no way to determine who might be haunting the place or how long the building has been experiencing ghostly activity, but there are certainly some strange things going on here.

Various areas of the building manifest eerie sounds and strange voices. Cold spots, some of which move and others that are stable, can be found at various locations throughout the structure. Late at night, after Vino's has closed, the staff routinely stack the chairs on top of the tables, so that they can mop the floors; frequently, when the morning staff arrives to open up, they find the chairs back on the floor and scattered around the room.

Vino's Brewpub is open seven days a week, Monday through Wednesday from 11:00 A.M. to 10:00 P.M., Thursday from 11:00 A.M. to 11:00 P.M., Friday from 11:00 A.M. to 12:00 A.M., Saturday from 11:30 A.M. to 12:00 A.M., and Sunday from 12:00 P.M. to 9:00 P.M.

FLORIDA

HERNANDO HERITAGE MUSEUM

601 Museum Court
Brooksville, FL 34601
(352) 799-0129
www.hernandohistoricalmuseum.com

Back in 1856, John May and his wife Marena built an impressive Renaissance Revival–style house. Towers, turrets, and sprawling verandas shoot out in every direction, and so, too, does the ghost of a little girl who remains in residence. The child in question was Jessie May Saxon, daughter of Marena May and her second husband, Frank Saxon. Jessie died at the age of 3, and her 150-year-old spirit still exhibits childlike tendencies. At night, she rearranges her toys inside their locked display cases, sometimes taking them out and scattering them on the floor, although the case remains securely locked. Her doll rests in her crib, but she dislikes having it to be moved. When it is, she throws the covers all over the room, and on one occasion, she completely disassembled the crib. Sometimes her small voice can be heard calling for her mother. Visitors to the house frequently feel like they are covered with cobwebs. Some people have reported a burning sensation on their skin and even develop red marks on the affected area. Glowing orbs have been seen and photographed outside the house. Staff members are so proud of their little ghost that they host weekly ghost tours.

Hernando Heritage Museum is open all year, Tuesday through Saturday from 12:00 P.M. to 3:00 P.M. Ghost tours are held every Friday and Saturday from 8:00 P.M. to 10:00 P.M. by reservation only. Admission fees apply.

THE ARTIST HOUSE
534 Eaton Street
Key West, FL 33040
(305) 296-3977 or (800) 582-7882
www.artisthousekeywest.com

Robert Eugene Otto was a well-known artist during the middle decades of the twentieth century. He grew up in Key West and inherited his family home, where he, and later his wife Ann, lived until he died in 1974. But that is not what this story is about. The tale and haunting of Gene Otto's former home revolves around a three-foot doll named Robert that was given to young Gene by his Jamaican nanny. Although the doll was a hideous thing, appearing neither human nor ape, Gene loved Robert and never let it out of his sight. Everyone else in the house was scared stiff of the horrid thing. Servants and family swore they heard Robert talking and laughing and caught fleeting glimpses of it running down the halls. Things began moving around inexplicably. When Gene's other toys were found destroyed, it was all blamed on Robert. An aunt insisted Robert be moved to the attic; the next night, she suffered a stroke and died.

Gene's parents passed away when he was in his twenties, and he and Robert lived alone until Gene got married. Even then, Robert was the couple's constant companion, sharing both their table and bed. After Gene and Anne died, the house, along with Robert, was sold to a new family. The new owners' ten-year-old daughter feared Robert, so her parents put him in the tower room. They subsequently awoke one night to find a vision of Robert standing at the foot of their bed holding a knife in his hand and laughing. That was the day they gave him to the East Martello Museum. Now Robert haunts both his old house and the museum. Guests at the old Otto house, now The Artist House bed-and-breakfast, still say they hear odd laughter and tiny footfalls running up and down the halls and see windows open and close by themselves. Passersby report seeing an apelike face staring out of the tower window, and some say that the spirit of poor Anne Otto remains trapped there with the spirit of the malignant doll. If you visit the nearby East Martello Museum and see Robert, make sure you introduce yourself and ask his permission before taking his picture. Many who did not have reportedly been followed home by his shadow.

The Artist House is a bed-and-breakfast inn that is open all year.

ERNEST HEMINGWAY HOME AND MUSEUM
907 Whitehead Street
Key West, FL 33040
(305) 294-1136
www.hemingwayhome.com

When Ernest Hemingway bought this lovely old house with its deep, sheltering eaves, it was already eighty years old and Hemingway was already one of America's most celebrated writers. Although Hemingway won both a Pulitzer Prize and a Nobel Prize, he suffered from deep depression and paranoia; these, combined with the side effects of electroshock therapy received during periodic incarcerations in a mental institution, contributed to his suicide in 1961. Shortly after his death, Hemingway's old home was made into a museum, and his ghost returned to this one and only place where he occasionally found solitude and happiness.

In his old studio, the lights go on and off by themselves and the sound of his old manual typewriter can be heard banging away late into the night. Hemingway's fully formed ghost has been seen walking along one of the house's balconies, as well as at his favorite bar, Sloppy Joe's, which is just down the street. On more than one occasion, Hemingway has been known to chat amiably with customers at Sloppy Joe's and is often seen walking out of the front door, although this may be no more than the wishful thinking of tourists who could easily mistake nearly any middle-aged man with a silver beard for the famous author.

Ernest Hemingway Home and Museum is open 365 days a year from 9:00 A.M. to 5:00 P.M. Admission fees apply.

Key West also has a ghost tour. Call them at (305) 294-9255 or visit their Web site at www.hauntedtours.com.

HERLONG MANSION HISTORIC INN AND GARDENS

402 NE Cholokka Boulevard
P. O. Box 667
Micanopy, FL 32667
(352) 466-3322 or (800) 437-5664
www.herlong.com

When Zetty Herlong and his wife Natalie inherited her family home in 1910, they completely rebuilt it, turning a simple house into a fine Greek Revival mansion, replete with massive Corinthian columns. It was a grand house and the Herlongs and their six children all loved it so much that after Zetty and Natalie died, the kids spent the next eighteen years fighting over ownership. Finally, daughter Inez bought out her surviving siblings, but soon after moving in she lapsed into a diabetic coma and died. In 1968, Inez's son sold the house. Over the ensuing years, a series of owners restored it and turned it into a lovely bed-and-breakfast inn.

It seems, however, that Inez loved the place so much that she just couldn't bear to leave. Throughout the long renovation process, workmen heard strange noises coming from the walls, the sound of the door to Inez's old room opening and closing, and footsteps on the stairs. They also saw lights coming from windows on the second floor and attic. Today, guests have occasionally been treated to all of these phenomena, along with a ghostly mist that moves up the stairs in the wake of the footfalls. Guests in the Inez Suite have also reported seeing the reflection of the good lady in the mirror, while others have seen her appear on the second-floor balcony, where she smiles before vanishing into thin air.

Herlong Mansion is a bed-and-breakfast inn that is open all year.

GEORGIA

WARREN HOUSE
102 West Mimosa Drive
Jonesboro, GA 30236
(770) 471-5553 or (770) 478-4800

When Guy Warren built his new house in 1840, he had no reason to assume it would ever be anything more than a quiet family home. For the next quarter of a century things worked out pretty much the way he assumed they would, but he had obviously not counted on the horrors of the Civil War. In late August and early September of 1864, Union and Confederate troops converged on Jonesboro in a struggle to control the local railroad line, for which Guy Warren worked as an agent. In the lead-up to the battle, Warren's house was commandeered by the Confederacy as a headquarters and field hospital, where hundreds of wounded were brought to convalesce. By September 2, the South had been routed and the Union took over the Warren house, which was again used as a hospital. The primitive medical treatment of the era, combined with an overwhelming number of wounded and dying, meant that dead bodies along with hundreds of amputated arms and legs were simply thrown out of the windows where they piled up around the house, sometimes three or four corpses deep until they could be buried.

Since then, the death agonies of these men have conspired to make this a very haunted house. The figure of a soldier, clutching a candle in one hand, sometimes peers out of the window. A bloodstain on the attic floor is said to resist all attempts at eradication. Doors open and slam shut of their own volition, orbs of light have been photographed floating through the house, and disembodied voices have been recorded on tape. The sound of military drums can sometimes be heard in the distance, but only when the listener is standing inside the house. Nearly as eerie as the hauntings themselves are the signatures of hundreds of wounded and dying soldiers that remain scrawled on the walls of the parlor.

Warren House is open for tours and special events by appointment only. Charges apply.

HAY HOUSE
934 Georgia Avenue
Macon, GA 31201
(478) 742-8155
www.georgiatrust.org/historic_sites/hay_house.htm

More properly referred to as the Johnston-Felton-Hay House, this wonderful Italian Renaissance home was built between 1855 and 1859 by local businessman William Johnston. Able to afford every modern convenience, Johnston had his house fitted with hot and cold running water, central heat, a ventilation system, and even speaking tubes connecting the rooms. The house itself was an architectural marvel covering 18,000 square feet on four floors and crowned by a three-story cupola. It was converted into a museum in 1974 and declared a National Historic Landmark.

No one knows the identity of the old woman who haunts the Hay House. Sometimes she seems to be just outside the back door, where she taps on the glass to get people's attention. When she is inside, she makes her presence known by footsteps in the halls, slamming doors, and moaning in the master bedroom. Visitors have often reported hearing the sound of someone breathing over their shoulder and cold spots are evident on the staircases. The local historical society that runs the house refuses to discuss the possibility that it is haunted, insisting that the Georgia Trust has a strict "no ghosts" policy.

Hay House is open Tuesday through Saturday from 10:00 A.M. to 4:00 P.M. and Sunday from 1:00 P.M. to 4:00 P.M. In January, February, July, and August, it is closed on Sundays. Tours last one hour. Admission fees apply. Special Behind the Scenes tours are available by advance reservation at an additional charge.

OLDE PINK HOUSE RESTAURANT
23 Abercorn Street
Savannah, GA 31401
(912) 232-4286

Over its nearly 250 years of existence, the Habersham house may never have seen any real tragedy, but it has suffered more indignity than any building should be forced to endure. The problems started in 1771, when James Habersham Jr. began building his home. Construction was interrupted while James was off fighting for American independence during the Revolutionary War and the British commandeered the partially finished house for their local headquarters. When Habersham returned home the work resumed. The brick structure was given a coat of white stucco, and the red dye in the bricks immediately began to bleed through, turning the house pink. No matter how many coats of paint he applied, the house stubbornly went back to pink. Just as stubbornly, the house survived the War of 1812, Savannah's great fire of 1820, and the Civil War, when it was commandeered as headquarters for Gen. William T. Sherman's officers. By the 1920s, the house was revamped for use as a restaurant, and acquiescing to its natural tendency, the owner painted it pink.

Still in use as a restaurant, called the Olde Pink House, the Habersham house has gathered an unlikely collection of ghosts. Most of the activity takes place in the basement piano bar, where James Habersham sometimes appears as an amazingly solid apparition who takes his place at the bar dressed in his Revolutionary War uniform, smiles at guests, and promptly vanishes. His apparition is so solid that many guests think he is a local reenactor, but strangely he only appears during the autumn and winter months. It seems that Habersham likes the candles on the tables and sometimes insists on relighting them after they have been put out for the night. Habersham's grandson, who appears as a man around sixty years old, also materializes in the basement bar before calmly walking out the door, heading to the local cemetery, and vanishing. A number of African American children also appear in the basement, where they can be seen playing dice in a hallway near the restrooms. These children were so fond of locking the bathroom doors that the management removed the locks. The children also playfully make a habit of untying guests' shoelaces. On the second floor is the unseen ghost of a woman who can be heard sobbing near the Purple Room, where swirling lights are sometimes seen.

Olde Pink House Restaurant is open all year long for dinner only. Doors open at 5:00 P.M.

KEHOE HOUSE
123 Habersham Street
Savannah, GA 31401
(912) 232-1020
www.kehoehouse.com

Little William Kehoe was only ten years old when his family emigrated from Ireland to the United States, but when he grew up he was determined to make something of himself. Apprenticing as a cast-iron molder, Kehoe went on to acquire his own foundry and made a good life for himself, his wife Annie, and their brood of children, ten of whom survived into adulthood. In 1892, Kehoe built a fine new thirteen-bedroom home for his flock, replacing the usual wooden gingerbread decoration with long-lasting cast-iron work. Eventually, the Kehoes all grew up and left home, and William and Annie died. The mansion became a funeral home, and then in 1992, when it was exactly one hundred years old, it was renovated into a hotel.

No one seems to know how long the hauntings have been going on there, but it seems that William, Annie, and at least some of their children remain in the house. The greatest amount of activity takes place in the rooms now known as 201 and 203. In 203, Annie has been seen sitting at her desk; occasionally, she sits down on the edge of the bed next to a sleeping guest. She has also been seen in 201, where she putters around, accompanied by the scent of roses. Room 201 is also the favorite haunt of a young Kehoe boy who has been known to gently touch the face of sleeping guests until they wake up, stare him eye-to-eye, and watch as he vanishes. Groups of children have been heard running down the halls and talking among themselves when there are no children staying at the hotel. Annie, too, has been seen in the third-floor hallway. Sometimes, one of the spirits rings the doorbell, and if their summons is not answered, all of the exterior doors in the house fly open simultaneously. To get away from the bustle of his ghostly family, William seems most comfortable sequestered away in his old study in the room just below the cupola. Here, late at night, soft lights are seen to go on and off, despite the fact that the room has not been used in years.

The Kehoe House is a bed-and-breakfast inn that is open all year. For reservations, call (800) 820-1020. For a nearby ghost tour in Savannah, contact Hauntings Tour at (912) 234-3571 or www .hauntingstour.com.

JULIETTE GORDON LOW BIRTHPLACE
10 East Oglethorpe Avenue
Savannah, GA 31401
(912) 233-4501
www.girlscouts.org/who_we_are/birthplace

Juliette Gordon Low, founder of the Girl Scouts of the U.S.A., was born and raised in this house, but it is her parents who are the center of our story. When Willie Gordon brought his new bride, Nelly, to his family home in Savannah in 1858, the venerable house was already nearly forty years old. Their family life was inevitably interrupted by the Civil War, when Willie left to serve as a general in the Georgia Hussars, but Nelly not only held the family together, she even managed to charm the notoriously irascible Gen. William T. Sherman into placing guards around her home. Unbelievably, Sherman even allowed her to send and receive mail. When the war ended, and Willie returned home, the Lows raised eight children and cared for each other until Willie died in 1912.

Five years later, as Nelly lay dying in her bedroom, her daughter-in-law Margaret was shocked senseless to see Willie walk out of his wife's room and down the stairs. The family butler confirmed that he came down and walked out the front door. Although Willie is almost never seen or heard from these days, Nelly now makes regular appearances to the Girl Scout Center staff and guests. Her footsteps are heard all over the house. She has been seen peering out of windows and spotted at the dining room table in her bathrobe. When she feels particularly happy, she treats people to a small recital on her old pianoforte, even though the instrument has not worked in decades.

Juliette Gordon Low Birthplace is open for tours Monday through Saturday from 10:00 A.M. to 4:00 P.M. and Sunday from 11:00 A.M. to 4:00 P.M. The site is closed on Wednesdays from November through February. Tours are free. For a nearby ghost tour in Savannah, contact Savannah Walks at (912) 238-9255 or www .savannahwalks.com.

KENTUCKY

LIBERTY HALL HISTORIC SITE
202 Wilkerson Street
Frankfort, KY 40601
(502) 227-2560 or (888) 516-5101
www.libertyhall.org

More than a stunning home, Liberty Hall is a wonderful panorama of one family's history. Built in 1796 by Sen. John Brown, in what was then the wilderness settlement of Frankfort, the house was designed by Brown's old law partner, Thomas Jefferson. Over the years, the famous and well-connected flocked to the Browns' home. In 1819 alone, guests included President James Monroe, Gen. Andrew Jackson, Col. Zachary Taylor, and the Marquis de Lafayette. During the Browns' long tenancy, there were two noteworthy tragedies that contributed to the house's spectral anomalies. In 1805, a Spanish opera singer visited Frankfort and stayed with the Brown family. During a party in her honor, the woman went for a walk and disappeared. No trace of her was ever found. Later, in 1817, Mrs. Brown's aunt, Margaret Varick, came for a visit, but the trip from New York proved too much for her and she died of a heart attack only days after arriving.

The Browns remained in the house until 1956, when it became a museum, but the hauntings had already been going on for many years. Aunt Margaret appeared only a few years after her death. Since then, she has been puttering around the house in a gray dress, doing small chores, smiling benignly at visitors and sometimes tucking them into bed at night. To this day she is known to do sewing and mending and often folds sheets and blankets. In her spare moments, she sits at a second-floor window watching people on the lawn. Twice she has been photographed coming down the stairs.

Two other ghosts haunt the lawn and grounds. One, a British soldier from the War of 1812, occasionally peeks in the windows of the house. The other is apparently the ghost of the unfortunate missing Spanish diva. On hot, humid nights her terrified ghost is seen running across the lawn, her mouth open in a silent scream. The staff of Liberty Hall is happy to discuss their long-dead companions.

Liberty Hall Historic Site is open May 26 through September 30, Tuesday through Saturday, from 10:00 A.M. to 5:00 P.M. Tours are given every ninety minutes. Admission fees apply. Discounts are available for groups of ten or more.

ASHLAND, THE HENRY CLAY ESTATE
120 Sycamore Road
Lexington, KY 40502
(859) 266-8581
www.henryclay.org

Like any true statesman, Henry Clay was a careful, patient man. In 1804, the year after he was first elected to the Kentucky State Legislature, he bought 125 acres of land and built a small house on it. Wings were added to the house in 1813 and 1815, and more land was acquired as it became available and affordable. Although Clay never achieved the presidency despite his burning ambition—running in 1824, 1832, 1840, 1844, and 1848—he spent a lifetime building his political career in the Senate and his beloved Ashland estate. When Clay died in 1852, the estate went to his son, James, who tore down the original house and rebuilt it as it appears today. The floor plan is identical to the original house, but the new building is by far more grand.

The Clay family remained at Ashland until 1948, when Senator Clay's great-granddaughter left the house and grounds to the Henry Clay Memorial Foundation, which turned it into a museum. Regardless of numerous changes, Clay never seems to have left his old house. From time-to-time the fully formed figure of the senator, decked out in a frock coat and still sporting his massive crown of white hair, still appears in the room he knew as the Red Parlor, which is now referred to as his study.

Ashland is open March through December on Saturday from 10:00 A.M. to 5:00 P.M. and Sunday from 1:00 P.M. to 5:00 P.M. The last tour begins at 4:00 P.M. The house is closed in January and open in February by appointment for groups of fifteen or more. Admission fees apply.

LOUDON HOUSE

Lexington Art League
209 Castlewood Drive
Lexington, KY 40505
(859) 254-7024
www.lexingtonartleague.org

Francis and Julia Hunt liked nice things. Luckily for them they could also afford them. When Francis married Julia, he was a young lawyer from a wealthy Lexington family and she was the socialite daughter of another well-to-do family. As a wedding present, Julia's folks gave the happy couple sixty acres of land. A few years later, John's father died and left him an inheritance of nearly $1 million—not bad for 1848. From this windfall, they spent a whopping $30,000 to build a truly grand mansion in the very latest Gothic Revival style. With steeply pitched roofs, towers, crenel-

lated turrets, lancet-toped windows, and porches popping out all
around, it must have set the staid neighbors on edge. In one sense
the story stops there. The Hunts lived out their lives, and the
house went through several owners before the city of Lexington
bought it in the 1920s. The building eventually became the home
of the Lexington Art League in 1984.

Of course, then there is the matter of the ghosts. Two spirits,
both female and dressed in Victorian clothing, continue to live in
the house. One of them, widely believed to be the spirit of Julia
Hunt, has been seen in the west wing of the house. The other
spirit, as yet unidentified, is seen in the old formal dining room
that also manifests a ghostly cat. In one of the bedrooms, now
used as an art studio, the scent of old-fashioned floral perfume
fills the air. The sound of 1890s music, punctuated by soft voices,
occasionally wafts through the house.

*Loudon House and the league's art gallery are open all year, Tues-
day through Friday from 10:00 A.M. to 4:00 P.M. and Saturday and
Sunday from 1:00 P.M. to 4:00 P.M. during exhibitions. Entry is free.*

DUPONT MANSION BED AND BREAKFAST
1317 South Fourth Street
Louisville, KY 40208
(502) 638-0045
www.dupontmansion.com

Before the middle of the nineteenth century, the du Pont family
had businesses all over the country and more money than normal
people can begin to imagine. In 1854, two of the du Pont brothers,
Alfred and Biederman, traveled to Louisville to explore new business possibilities, and in short order they had established a paper
mill and a gunpowder manufacturing plant.

In 1870, Biederman bought a fine, Italianate house and decided
he would build a similar one to accommodate family and business
associates when they came to town. Alfred preferred to live at a
local hotel, mostly because of its proximity to Louisville's brothels,
but he often went to the new family guesthouse for business meetings and to entertain friends. The du Pont family guesthouse was

sold in 1886, and seven years later, Alfred was shot in the chest and killed by a madam who was pregnant with his child but refused to be bought off with du Pont money. A few years after Alfred's death, the old du Pont house was divided into apartments and slowly sank into disrepair, until by the 1990s, it was almost beyond saving. At this point a wealthy couple stepped in, completely restored the house, and opened it as a bed-and-breakfast complete with its own ghost.

No one is certain how long Alfred du Pont has been living at his old family gathering place, but he has been in evidence at least since the renovations began. He mostly appears, in full evening clothes, near the bottom of the main staircase, sometimes sporting a bloody hole in his shirtfront. He also appears most often to women, a few of whom claim the still-lecherous Alfred has breathed down their necks and touched them on the bottom. Some people never learn.

DuPont Mansion Bed and Breakfast is open all year and occasionally hosts what it calls "ghostly specials." Check their Web site for times and events.

SOUTHGATE HOUSE
24 East 3rd Street
Newport, KY 41071
(859) 431-2201
www.southgatehouse.com

A nightclub is a likely place to find a wide variety of interesting spirits, but they normally come out of a bottle, not out of the walls. Of course, Southgate House wasn't always a nightclub. When Richard Southgate build his new house in 1814, he was already a lawyer and state representative, and he was about to be elected as the United States senator from Kentucky, so he knew exactly what he could get away with legally. To keep construction costs down, Southgate used the forced labor of British POWs being held in Newport during the War of 1812. No doubt it was a grand house and the Southgate family remained there for a full three generations. In 1914, the house was sold to the Knights of

Columbus, and in more recent years, it has become a nightclub, performing arts center, and art gallery.

Three ghosts have been here for as long as anyone can remember. One ghost, a female, occasionally plays the piano and opens and closes the front door. Another spirit, a young boy about six years old, has been seen running all over the building. The third ghost, a Confederate soldier in uniform, appears on the second-floor landing and in the men's bathroom. It is assumed that it is this same soldier's laughter that is heard in the first-floor bar, and he has been accused of making customer's drinks slide across the table and into their laps. Unfortunately, the most active parts of the building are off-limits to customers, and constant human activity makes catching glimpses of the spectral dead difficult at the best of times.

Southgate House is open evenings for live performances. The third floor is an art gallery, which is open from 3:00 P.M. to 7:00 P.M., seven days a week. Check the Web site for performance times and schedules.

LOUISIANA

T'FRERES BED AND BREAKFAST
1905 Verot School Road
Lafayette, LA 70508
(337) 984-9347 or (800) 984-9347
www.tfreres.com

This lovely old 1880s Colonial Revival house had many owners before it was turned into a bed-and-breakfast. The records of its past are a bit sketchy, and many of the owners' names have been lost, but it seems that one of those who lived here was a young widow whose first name was Amelie.

The precise circumstances surrounding Amelie's death remain in dispute. The only thing we know for certain is that she drowned in the well. Whether she slipped and fell in accidentally, was pushed, or committed suicide remains a mystery, but it may be one of the contributing factors in her continued haunting of T'Freres House.

After Amelie's body was recovered, the Roman Catholic Church declared her a suicide and therefore ineligible for last rites and burial in hallowed ground. Evidently this decision does not rest well with Amelie. Her entity has been seen, wandering through the house and grounds, wearing a rose-colored dress. She opens and closes doors, rattles pots and pans in the kitchen, and moves furniture and other objects from place to place. Occasionally, she bangs out a few notes on the old piano. One past owner credits her with waking his family one night when a fire had broken out in the house and thereby saving their lives. Amelie's own life may have been inexplicably cut short, but she seems concerned that a similar fate should not befall others who live in her home.

T'Freres Bed and Breakfast is open all year and operates a restaurant with cuisine that is both renowned and scrumptious.

BEAUREGARD-KEYES HOUSE
1113 Chartres Street
New Orleans, LA 70130
(504) 523-7257
www.bkhouse.org

This lovely southern mansion is one of the most unusual entries in this book, because while everyone agrees it is haunted, the precise nature of the haunting is wildly disputed. The house gets its name from its two most famous residents: Confederate general Pierre G. T. Beauregard, famous for a stunning victory at Bull Run and a shattering defeat at Shiloh; and author Frances Parkinson Keyes, known for her novels set in Louisiana, who was the last resident.

When Keyes passed away in 1970, the house became a museum and, with that, the dispute over the hauntings began.

The staff admits that an unseen presence moves furniture on the second floor and that they hear the sound of fiddle music and dancing in the ballroom. Most interestingly, they also say there are two ghosts, but they insist that neither of them were human. One is the spirit of Keyes's cocker spaniel Lucky, and the other is the entity of an unknown cat the staff has named Caroline. While animal ghosts are fairly rare—and two in the same house is almost unheard of—they can't compete with the other ghost story, the one the staff adamantly denies. This alternate haunting was first reported before the house became a museum and continues to be told by those who pass by the house at night and pause to peer through the windows. These witnesses insist that on rare occasions, General Beauregard and his troops, replete with horses, mules, flags, and banners, appear out of the paneling in the hallway leading toward the ballroom. Charging along the hall, the soldiers are chopped to pieces by musket fire, cannonballs, and grapeshot, swirling away in a cloud of smoke and shattered limbs. How General Beauregard's ignoble defeat at the Battle of Shiloh came to this house in New Orleans remains a mystery. Strange that none of the ghost stories include the shooting deaths of four Mafia thugs, which took place in the house in the 1920s.

Beauregard-Keyes House is open all year, Monday through Saturday from 10:00 A.M. to 3:00 P.M. It is closed on legal holidays. Admission fees apply.

COLUMNS HOTEL
3811 St. Charles Avenue
New Orleans, LA 70115
(504) 899-9308 or (800) 899-0506
www.thecolumns.com

Strangely, none of the trauma, violence, unfinished business, or bad karma usually associated with spectral activity seems to be in any way attached to this grand old southern home. The house was built in 1883 by a wealthy tobacco merchant named Simon Hernsheim, who lived in the house with his family only until 1889.

Over the next few decades, it was transformed from a private residence into a very upscale boardinghouse and then into a hotel. In 1982, it was listed in the National Register of Historic Places.

So where did the three spirits that haunt the Columns Hotel come from? Frankly, no one knows. One of the entities appears as a lady in a white dress, who most often appears in the ballroom and outside in the garden. Then there is the little girl who wanders around the third floor and the gentleman who occasionally pops up to look in on the guests. They may not have been a family in life, but we hope they get along well in the afterlife; they certainly all seem to get on well with the living.

Columns Hotel is open all year. Even if you do not plan to stay, you can enjoy their Sunday jazz brunch or a drink in the lounge. Brunch reservations are recommended.

LALARIE HOUSE
1140 Royal Street
New Orleans, LA 70116

No listing of haunted houses in New Orleans would be complete without a mention of the notorious Lalarie House. Dr. Louis Lalarie and his wife Delphine bought their home in 1832 and turned it into one of the social centers of a city that reveled in its high society. The house was grand and the host and hostess were gracious, but evidently their polish and gentility was only a glittering facade. While virtually all wealthy people in the South owned slaves at that time, the law still demanded fair treatment for those held as property. The Lalaries, however, particularly Delphine, were evidently brutal and cruel beyond words. A little more than a year after the Lalaries moved into their house, a neighbor heard a scream and saw Delphine chasing a young slave girl around the house's balcony with a whip. Terrified, the girl jumped to her death. Investigating authorities confiscated the Lalaries' slaves and fined them $500. The Lalaries bought their slaves back the following year. After a fire in the house, the brigade discovered seven malnourished and mistreated slaves chained in a horribly overcrowded room near the kitchen. The Lalaries escaped prosecution by leaving New Orleans, but their house soon gained the reputation of being haunted.

According to later newspaper and eyewitness accounts, the sounds of clanking chains and screams continue to emanate from the old Lalarie mansion. Misty shapes also appear, and several times these apparitions have been caught on film. Eventually, the mansion was converted into luxury apartments, and while the house remains a private residence, it is certainly true that it has changed hands, and tenants, more frequently than normal.

Lalarie House is not open to the public, but there are several ghost walks and tours in New Orleans, and they all stop there; see the Web sites for Big Easy Tours (www.BigEasyTours.us), Haunted History Tours (www.hauntedhistorytours.com), or New Orleans Spirit Tours (www.neworleanstours.net).

MYRTLES PLANTATION
7747 U.S. Highway 61
P.O. Box 1100
St. Francisville, LA 70775
(225) 635-6277 or (800) 809-0565
www.myrtlesplantation.com

Standing in a grove of ancient oaks dripping with Spanish moss, the Myrtles Plantation belies its often violent past, looking the very image of antebellum southern gentility. Looks, of course, can be deceiving. When Gen. David "Whiskey Dave" Bradford built this twenty-two-room mansion in 1796, he already had a price on his head for his part in the Whiskey Rebellion of 1794.

While Bradford lived out his life peacefully, the same cannot be said for the dozen or so people who died violently here, and that does not include the restless spirits from the Native American burial ground on which the plantation was built. The most active ghost is that of a black governess named Chloe, who was also the lover of Judge Clark Woodruff, one of Bradford's sons-in-law. It seems that Woodruff caught Chloe listening in on a private conversation and cut off her ear. To get her revenge, Chloe baked a poisoned cake and served it at the birthday party of one of

Woodruff's daughters. Two of the girls and Mrs. Woodruff died, and Chloe was lynched by the other slaves.

Today, Chloe appears in a flowing robe and bright green turban and often disturbs sleeping guests by staring intently at them until they waken. It seems likely that Chloe's two young victims account for the ghosts of two little blond girls who play on the verandas, peek in the windows, and sometimes creep into guests' rooms. We are unsure if it is one of the girls who bounces unseen on the freshly made beds, but a clearly visible spirit maid straightens them out again.

Then there is William Winter, who bought Myrtles in 1860. In 1871, Winter was shot and killed by an unknown assailant as he walked out the front door. Staggering back into the house, he made it halfway up the stairs before dying in his wife's arms. Today his invisible ghost can be heard reenacting his final moments. Myrtles also has a Confederate soldier who paces the front porch, a voodoo priestess whose chanting can be heard, an unknown ballerina in a black tutu, and a number of slaves who report to work from the graveyard. Last, but far from least, is the stark naked apparition of a lovely young Native American girl who lounges in the gazebo. Myrtles and its ghosts have been featured in dozens of magazines and television shows.

Myrtles Plantation is a bed-and-breakfast inn and is open all year. In addition to overnight accommodations, they have a full-service restaurant open to the public. They also conduct tours of the house daily between 9:00 A.M. and 5:00 P.M. and mystery tours are held every Friday and Saturday evening. Charges apply.

MISSISSIPPI

ERROLTON
216 3rd Avenue
Columbus, MS 39701

William Weaver wanted his family to be happy, and he had the money to accommodate their wishes. Around 1848, he built the grand home now known as Errolton, and here, he and his wife raised their family. If parents are allowed to have favorites among their children, Weaver's favorite was his daughter Nellie. She was a happy girl and so in love with her home and family that she etched her name into one of the window panes in the south parlor. In 1878, Nellie married a man named Charles Tucker, who moved into Errolton, had one child with Nellie, and then promptly ran off. Now alone, Nellie opened a small private school, but money was tight and the house slowly fell into disrepair. Nellie stubbornly remained in her family home until she died in 1934 at the age of eighty in a small fire.

During the early 1950s, the house underwent a major restoration, during which the pane of glass with Nellie's name etched in it was accidentally broken. The glass was replaced, and not long later, one of the caretakers noticed that in one corner the name Nellie had magically reappeared in the glass. Nellie never makes herself seen, but visitors to Errolton say they can feel her presence.

Errolton is open to the public on an irregular basis. Call the Columbus Convention and Visitors Bureau at (662) 329-1191 or (800) 327-2686, or visit their Web site, www.columbus-ms.info, for specific dates, times, and fees. During the last weekend of October, Columbus offers a Ghosts and Legends tour.

CEDAR GROVE MANSION INN AND RESTAURANT
2200 Oak Street
Vicksburg, MS 39180
(601) 636-1000 or (800) 862-1300
www.cedargroveinn.com

When John Klein decided to get married at the age of thirty, he was already a successful jeweler and architect and had investments in lumber, banking, and cotton. His bride-to-be, Elizabeth Day, was just sixteen. As a gift to his bride, John designed and built a big house in 1852 on a bluff overlooking the Yazoo River and named it Cedar Grove. Complete with columns, verandas, porches, and gardens, the house was a fine home in which to raise their ten children. Like any family, the Kleins had some rough times. During the Civil War, when John was off fighting for the Confederacy, Vicksburg was besieged by Union troops, but Gen. William T. Sherman, who happened to be a distant cousin of Elizabeth's, hustled her to safety and preserved her house by turning it into a Union hospital. The Kleins also lost four of their ten children; two died as infants, one young girl died of a childhood illness, and a son accidentally dropped his rifle on the back stairs where it discharged and killed him at seventeen. In 1919, the Kleins sold Cedar Grove, and a later female inhabitant committed suicide in the old ballroom.

By the time Cedar Grove was converted into one of the South's grandest bed-and-breakfasts, it had accumulated quite a number of ghosts. In what was once John Klein's private parlor, guests sometimes smell his pipe tobacco. Wife Elizabeth can occasionally be seen coming down the stairs. Some of their children are in the house, too. The sound of a baby crying can sometimes be heard, and the spirit of a lost and confused little girl sometimes ascends the same stairs her mother descends. The footsteps of the son can still be heard on the back stairs where he died. A shadowy figure, assumed to be the woman who committed suicide, has been spotted, as have several Civil War–era soldiers.

Cedar Grove is a bed-and-breakfast with a restaurant open to the public. There are occasional tours of the property; check their Web site for tour dates and times.

MCRAVEN TOUR HOME
1445 Harrison Street
Vicksburg, MS 39180
(601) 636-1663
www.mcraventourhome.com

The physical history of the McRaven house is almost as haphazard and checkered as the string of tragedies that have taken place there. The original portion of the house was built by the McRaven family in 1797. In 1836, it was purchased by Sheriff Steven Howard, who added what is now the central portion of the house. Only a few months after Howard bought the house, his fifteen-year-old wife, Mary Elizabeth, died in childbirth. Less than a year later, his surrounding property was used as a stopping point on the Cherokee Trail of Tears, part of the brutal, forced migration of thousands of Native Americans in the 1830s from lands in the South.

During the Civil War, the house, then owned and enlarged by John Bobb, was used as a Confederate field hospital and, later, as Union headquarters during the occupation of Vicksburg. Here, Union officers employed the services of James McPherson as a liaison between Union occupiers and the townsfolk. One night McPherson failed to return from his rounds, but a few weeks later, his bloodied, dripping-wet ghost appeared to his commanding officer to explain he had been murdered and thrown into the Yazoo River. Only weeks later, John Bobb got into a heated argument with a group of Union soldiers, in which he was beaten to death.

Since then, at least six more people have died in the house, although all of these deaths were peaceful. After the death of the last owner, Ella Murray, in 1960, the house was opened to the public as a private museum, but the ghosts of the past continue to linger. Mary Elizabeth Howard is seen in the dining room and on the staircase, and she evidently turns on and off the light next to her old bed. Another owner, William Murray, has appeared on the staircase, while the apparitions of both Union and Confederate soldiers have been seen inside and on the grounds; some visitors report being touched and shoved as they tour the house. Other phenomena include phantom mists, distant mumbling voices, floating orbs, and strange smells. The house has been investigated several times and was exorcised in 1991, but it seems to have done little to deter the numerous guests from the past.

McRaven Tour Home was on the market when this book was written, but it remains open for tours by special appointment.

WAVERLY MANSION
1852 Waverly Mansion Road
West Point, MS 39773
(662) 494-1399 or (800) 920-3533

George Hampton Young was the rarest of gentlemen—a good, kind man who was also very lucky and successful. When Young built Waverly in 1852, he not only made it big enough to accommodate his wife and ten children, all of whom survived to adulthood, but to serve as a center for local social life. Almost every week there were balls and dances in the house, and friends were always welcome at Young's table. During the Civil War and Reconstruction era, Young opened his house to many who had been left homeless and destitute.

By 1913, the Youngs had either died off or departed, and Waverly slowly deteriorated to a shadow of its formerly lovely self. Not everyone was gone, however. During this period, neighbors and passersby often heard the sounds of faint music and happy voices coming from the ballroom. Others saw the spirit of Maj. John Pytchlyn, who had lived nearby long before Waverly was built, riding bareback near the overgrown grounds. In 1962, after being abandoned for half a century, the house was rescued and restored by private owners who soon became aware of the house's uninvited inhabitants. Major Pytchlyn was still there, as were the sounds from the ballroom. There was also the face of George Young himself, who occasionally appeared in one of the mirrors. The most frequent ghost through the years has been an unknown little girl of about five or six years old. Appearing in a long nightgown, the poor child wanders around the house calling "mama" and following people in the forlorn hope that they will help her find her lost mother. Eventually she gives up in frustration, vanishing into a mist. Exhausted by her wanderings, she sometimes lays down on the bed in a room kept exclusively for her use and her small impression can be seen on the bedspread.

Waverly Mansion is a private home, but the owners generously keep it open for tours all year, except on legal holidays, by appointment only.

NORTH CAROLINA

BILTMORE VILLAGE INN
119 Dodge Street
Asheville, NC 28803
(828) 274-8707 or (866) 274-8779
www.biltmorevillageinn.com

Sometimes, lives that seem destined for only the best things go inexplicably awry. Samuel H. Reed came from a wealthy family with good social connections. His father, Joseph, owned more than twelve hundred acres of good land just outside Asheville, along with a sawmill, carding mill, and gristmill. Also among his extensive holdings were a brickyard, meat market, store, and hotel. When Sam was born in 1851, his family was already able to provide anything he might need or want, including a law degree and financial security.

When Joseph Reed died in 1884, thirty-three-year-old Sam inherited a large portion of his holdings, and this only added to the security provided by his being a lawyer in the employ of the massively wealthy Vanderbilt family. For Samuel and his wife Jessie, the future should have held only good things, but by the time they built their house in 1892, they had already lost several children; only four of their nine offspring would live beyond infancy. In late 1904, Jessie Reed died, and six months later, fifty-three-year-old Sam followed her. Three of their surviving children were sent to live with relatives, while the eldest, Wingate, lived at college. The big old house was subdivided into apartments, and over the decades it changed hands many times.

During the 1960s, the house stood abandoned. Ten years later, it was threatened with condemnation and demolition. By 2000, however, it had been largely refurbished and opened as a bed-and-breakfast inn. Somewhere along the way, the long-absent and long-dead Reeds seem to have returned to their home. By the 1970s, the sound of heavy footsteps was heard going up and down the old servants' stairs, and since then the activity has only increased. The doors to two guestrooms open and close by themselves and lights go on and off, but the ghosts' favorite activity seems to be playing billiards. In the gameroom, the sound of racked pool balls being split can be heard at all hours of the day and night. The ghosts seem particularly happy when they have real balls to play with, but if none are available, phantom balls seem to work just fine.

Biltmore Village Inn is a bed-and-breakfast and is open all year.

HAMMOCK HOUSE
Hammock Lane (off of Front Street)
Beaufort, NC 28516

Considering that its history reaches back more than three hundred years and the amount of violence that has taken place here, it is hardly surprising that Hammock House is considered haunted. We don't know who built the house, but a date carved into one of the timbers tells us it was built in 1700. We know that Robert Turner owned and operated the property as an inn in 1713 and that one of his semiregular guests was no less than the notorious pirate Edward "Blackbeard" Teach. It seems that during one stay, while his ship *Queen Anne's Revenge* was being refitted nearby, Black-beard brought with him an eighteen-year-old captive to serve as his unwilling wife. By the time he left he had tired of the girl and hanged her from an oak on the house's lawn. Her ghost is still said to be heard screaming and choking at the site of her death.

Only a few decades later, in 1747, the house was owned by a British naval captain named Richard Russell, who returned home after an extended sea voyage to find his wife dancing with a man in the parlor. Flying into a rage, Russell chased the man up the stairs, drew his sword, and ran the stranger through. Imagine his surprise when he found out the man was his wife's brother. The tragedies continued through the Civil War, when Union forces occupied Beaufort in 1862. The now-abandoned house was to be used to quarter Union troops. One evening three soldiers on reconnaissance wandered toward the house and disappeared; their skeletal remains were discovered in 1915 by workers digging near the back porch. No one knows who killed them, but their restless spirits are said to remain tied to the spot of their death. Because Hammock House has always remained in private hands and closed to the public, the exact nature and frequency of the hauntings, with the exception of Blackbeard's victim, is unknown.

Hammock House is not open to the public, but is included in local tours given by the Beaufort Historical Association, ((800) 575-7483; beauforthistoricsite.org/tours.htm) and Beaufort Ghost Walk ((252) 772-9925; www.tourbeaufort.com/ghostwalk.htm)

DUKE MANSION
400 Hermitage Road
Charlotte, NC 28207
(704) 714-4400
www.dukemansion.com

This fine, colonial mansion was built in 1915 by tobacco tycoon James B. Duke, best remembered for founding Duke University. The Dukes' residency lasted only fourteen years, and the house has subsequently changed hands at least five times. The only owner who contributes to our story is Jon Avery.

Avery's wife suffered a mental breakdown and while she was confined to a hospital, Avery met and fell in love with another woman. Being an honorable man, Avery was unwilling to abandon or divorce his wife, and his lover broke off the relationship. Desperate not to lose his new love, Avery convinced her to meet him once a year at midnight in the circular garden near the house. Apparently they met twice before the woman became engaged to another man. Not wanting to disappoint Avery but anxious not to encourage him, she decided to take one of her female friends along with her to the next meeting. When Avery arrived at the appointed time, he seemed not to see the women, and when his friend reached out to grab his sleeve, her hand went right through him. Jon Avery had died only weeks earlier, but seemed unwilling to disappoint his friend even in death. The Duke Mansion was restored and converted into a bed-and-breakfast in 1989, but no one knows whether Jon Avery still keeps his appointments as his ghost has not been seen in recent years.

The Duke Mansion Bed & Breakfast is open all year.

MORDECAI HOUSE
Capitol Area Preservation Society
1 Mimosa Street
Raleigh, NC 27604
(919) 857-4364
www.nps.gov/nr/travel/raleigh/mor.htm

Moses Mordecai was one of the first Jews to take up residence in Raleigh. He established a law office and married Margaret Lane, one of the daughters of Joel Lane, who had helped establish Raleigh. When Joel Lane died Moses and Margaret inherited his house, which had been built in 1785, and largely remodeled it. The Lanes and Mordecais retained ownership of the house until 1967, when it was purchased by a local preservation society and restored as a museum along with several other buildings in the immediate area.

The house seems to support only one ghost, a female member of the Mordecai-Lane family, but her apparitions are so startlingly lifelike that they make her nearly indistinguishable from the living. Identified by staff as Margaret Mordecai, a later descendant and namesake of Moses Mordecai's wife, the ghost appears as an attractive young woman dressed in a pleated black skirt, white blouse, and black necktie typical of the first decade of the twentieth century. Margaret never bothers anyone, but simply goes about her business, moving from room to room, appearing and disappearing at will.

Mordecai House is open all year, Tuesday through Saturday from 10:00 A.M. to 4:00 P.M. and Sunday from 1:00 P.M. to 4:00 P.M. It is closed on major holidays. Admission fees apply.

OKLAHOMA

STONE LION INN
1016 West Warner Avenue
Guthrie, OK 73044
(405) 282-0012
www.stonelioninn.com

While the owners and staff of many haunted houses deny the issue of their resident spirits, or at least avoid it, the owners of the old F. E. Houghton mansion, now the Stone Lion Inn, seem delighted with their ghosts. When F. E. Houghton built his massive Greek Revival mansion in 1907, he was the proud owner of an oil company, several stores, and the first automobile dealership in Oklahoma. He was also the proud father of a brood of six children. The family had been in the house only a few years when the Houghton's eight-year-old daughter, Augusta, contracted whooping cough. At the time, this was a life-threatening illness, so medical attention was paramount. Although the disease did not kill little Augusta, the wrong medicine administered by a careless maid did. When the family sold the property in the early 1920s, it became in rapid succession a boardinghouse and then a funeral home.

In 1986, the property was converted into a bed-and-breakfast, and by that time it was already experiencing numerous manifestations. The most frequent occurrences are all connected to Augusta, whose small footsteps can be heard going up and down the wooden back stairs and running along the halls. She also has a penchant for playing with other children's toys, dragging them out from where they are stored, and leaving them scattered across the floor. Although no one has seen Augusta, some overnight guests report feeling her small hand touch them on the cheek early in the morning. Augusta's father, F. E. Houghton, has also been spotted here. His visible specter has been seen in the basement, and both the smell and curling smoke of his cigars have been witnessed in the first-floor rooms of the house.

Stone Lion Inn is a bed-and-breakfast and is open all year. They offer full dinners and host regular murder mystery evenings and occasional overnight ghost hunts, all open to the public with advance reservations.

GILCREASE MUSEUM
1400 North Gilcrease Museum Road
Tulsa, OK 74127
(918) 596-2700 or (888) 655-2278
www.gilcrease.org

In 1900, the U.S. government dissolved the Creek Indian reservation twenty miles southwest of Tulsa and divided the land among the Creek people. Among the recipients was ten-year-old Thomas Gilcrease, one-eighth Creek, who received 160 acres of dry, dusty land. Five years later, oil was discovered there, and before he was twenty, Gilcrease was a multimillionaire. Three years after that, in 1913, he and his wife, Belle, were shopping for a new house when they spotted a one-story, nine-room house built of native stone on an eighty-acre plot of land. The house was only one year old and the owner had no thought of selling, but Gilcrease's wallet convinced him otherwise.

For the next thirty years, Gilcrease managed his oil company while collecting Western and Native American art, filling every spare inch of his house with it. By 1941, the collection was so extensive that the old barn and garages had to be converted into art galleries. In 1943, Gilcrease added a second story to the house and temporarily turned it into an orphanage for parentless Indian children. But by 1949, he had moved back in, keeping many of the children there. When Gilcrease died in 1962, he willed his house, property, and one of the world's largest collections of Western American art and artifacts to the people of Tulsa. But, always having been a hands-on sort of guy, he decided to hang around his house just to make sure his collection was managed properly.

Late at night, when all the tourists have gone, Gilcrease still wanders through his art museum, a habit that causes a high turnover in night watchmen. The rest of the time he wanders through nearly every room of his house and the adjoining gardens. The ghosts of seven Native American children remain here, too, but they are far too well-mannered to bother anyone; they just run around and play quietly in the sunny gardens. Another male ghost is present, and his identity is anybody's guess, but he seems to feel right at home with Gilcrease and the children.

Gilcrease Museum is open all year, Tuesday through Sunday from 10:00 A.M. to 5:00 P.M. It is closed on Mondays and Christmas Day. Admission fees apply.

SOUTH CAROLINA

BATTERY CARRIAGE HOUSE INN
20 South Battery
Charleston, SC 29401
(843) 727-3100 or (800) 775-5575
www.batterycarriagehouse.com

When this grand, five-story southern mansion was built in 1845, Charleston was the most prosperous city in the South. The owner, Samuel Stevens, was a money lender and cotton futures trader who displayed his wealth with an easy assurance. In 1859, Stevens sold the house only months before the secession crisis. From the firing on Fort Sumter on April 12, 1861, until the end of the Civil War four years later, Charleston was a constant war zone. Directly across the street from this grand house stood the defending cannon emplacements. Return fire from Union gunships and artillery caused the entire civilian population to evacuate, and the Stevens house and its adjoining carriage house were used as dormitories for weary Confederate soldiers.

In 1870, the deteriorated, shell-damaged house was sold to Col. Richard Lathers, who repaired the damage but was driven out of town for his Union sympathies. For the next hundred years, the house slowly deteriorated. By the 1920s, the carriage house had been converted into a hotel, noted for wild parties; twenty years later, the rooms were rented by the hour rather than by the night. The final straw came in 1989 in the form of Hurricane Hugo. Battered and worn, the house stood empty until its 1992 restoration, when a portion of it and the carriage house became a bed-and-breakfast.

With such a violent and decadent past, it's a wonder there aren't more ghosts here. The most frightening is the headless torso that appears in Room 8. Open-shirted and wearing a coarse coat, the unknown spirit is terrifying to behold, and his heavy breathing has frightened more than one guest. Another ghost, known as "the Gentleman," is apparently the college-aged son of the Simonds family who owned the house in the early twentieth century; he committed suicide by jumping off the carriage house roof. This slender young man comes to Room 10 and sometimes appears fairly solid and at other times is no more than a shadow moving through walls and doors. In Room 3, glowing orbs congregate in the sitting area in impressive numbers and move around the room. All of the ghosts have been photographed.

Battery Carriage House Inn is a bed-and-breakfast and is open all year. Tours of the main mansion are available through the main desk.

POOGAN'S PORCH RESTAURANT

72 Queen Street
P.O. Box 534
Charleston, SC 29401
(843) 577-2337
www.poogansporch.com

The old St. Armand house is now a charmingly upscale restaurant with the unusual name of Poogan's Porch. Poogan never owned the house or the restaurant, but he did spent his later years lounging on the porch watching the conversion of this 1888 house into a restaurant and generally getting in the way. Poogan, you see, was a scruffy neighborhood dog, and when he died in 1979, he was buried in the yard of the restaurant that already bore his name.

The house had originally belonged to two spinster schoolteachers, Elizabeth and Zoe St. Armand. They lived in the big house most of their lives. After Elizabeth died in 1945, Zoe remained in the house alone, until her health deteriorated to the point that friends moved her to a nursing home. When she died in 1954, the house and its contents were auctioned off. In 1974, the house was on the market again, and the Ball family, looking for a place to open a restaurant, bought it.

Along with faulty plumbing and outdated wiring came two unexpected perks—a big, shaggy dog who liked to sun himself on the porch and the ghost of Zoe St. Armand. The Balls first heard about Zoe from the owners of the neighboring Mills House Hotel, where staff and guests would see Zoe in a black dress, waving from a second-floor window. Inside Poogan's Porch, Zoe's ghost has been spotted walking around and then disappearing abruptly, and she is understandably blamed for the occasional flying saucepan in the kitchen. Floating, glowing orbs have been photographed on the porch and on the gable of the roof. Poogan, too, has been spotted. While the owners and staff deny that their old friend has come back, guests lounging on his favorite porch claim to have felt an invisible animal brush against their legs.

Poogan's Porch Restaurant is open 365 days a year. Lunch is served Monday through Friday from 11:30 A.M. to 2:30 P.M. Saturday and Sunday brunch is served from 9:00 A.M. to 3:00 P.M. Dinner is served every day from 5:00 P.M. to 9:30 P.M. Reservations are recommended. One of Charleston's two ghost walks meets next door at the Mills House Hotel, Monday through Saturday. For information, call (843) 577-5931 or visit their Web site at www.ghostwalk.net.

MEETING STREET INN
173 Meeting Street
Charleston, SC 29401
(843) 723-1882 or (800) 842-8022
www.meetingstreetinn.com

When the old Charleston Theater burned to the ground in 1861, the event went nearly unnoticed. Considering that the embattled city was already under siege by Union forces and more than six hundred buildings were destroyed in the terrible fire of December 12 and 13, the loss of one theater was hardly critical. In 1874, the land where the theater had formerly stood became the site of a new building, a combination saloon, restaurant, beer and wine store, and home for the family of the business' owner, Adolph Tiefenthal. The Tiefenthal family owned and operated the businesses for fifteen years, and over the following century, the building was used for such varied purposes as a brewery, ice company, antique store, auto parts store, dental equipment supplier, liquor store, and bicycle rental business. In 1981, the long, narrow, fifty-six-room, shotgun-style building was renovated and restored to become the Meeting Street Inn

Among the establishment's permanent guests are at least two members of the Tiefenthal family, who have remained in the building through more than a century of changing uses and ownership. Room 303 is home to an unseen entity that seems very particular about its privacy. The door to 303 sometimes refuses to unlock, and even when it does, the burliest members of staff sometimes find it impossible to open. On at least one occasion, when the staff prepared to batter down the door, it simply swung open by itself. The ghost of Room 107 is both less confrontational and more visible. Assumed to be the spirit of the late Mrs. Tiefenthal, she occasionally materializes at the foot of the bed. From the waist up, she appears real, but from there down she slowly fades away to nothingness. A friendly, nonthreatening soul, she seems unaware of the living and only turns away, floats to the door, opens it, and disappears.

Meeting Street Inn is a bed-and-breakfast that is open all year. Charleston has two ghost walks. The first is listed under the previous entry. For information on the other one, the Ghosts of Charleston, call (800) 854-1670 or visit their Web site at www.tour charleston.com.

TENNESSEE

BELL WITCH CAVE AND BELL CABIN
430 Keysburg Road
Adams, TN 37010
(615) 696-3055
www.bellwitchcave.com

The story of the Bell Witch and the haunting of the John Bell family is probably the best known supernatural incident in American history. In 1817, the family of John Bell began hearing knocking and scratching sounds coming from the walls of their log cabin. Over the weeks and months to come the intensity of the hauntings increased; blankets were pulled from beds and family members were slapped and beaten with increasing ferocity. Most of the spirit's attention fell on John Bell himself and his eleven-year-old daughter, Elizabeth. Eventually the entity began speaking, and for the next three years it was seldom quiet—shrieking, cursing, and bragging about what it would do to the Bells. Every day the invisible being bedeviled the Bells and it even extended its visitations to those in the surrounding town of Red River (now Adams). When Gen. Andrew Jackson and some of his men came to investigate in 1819, two of his men were thrashed senseless by the ghost and Jackson fled in terror.

Before John Bell died in 1821, a death reportedly hastened by the spirit, a vague explanation of the events had been assembled. Most believed the spirit came from a cave located on the Bell property and was controlled by Kate Batts, a suspected witch with whom John Bell had argued. The Bell family is long gone, but some aspects of the spirit linger on in the Bell Witch Cave, where visitors have been dragged to the ground by unseen arms that encircle their chests and pull them downward. Other visitors have been slapped so hard by an invisible hand that red welts raise on their faces. Footsteps, rasping breaths, and whispering are heard in the cave, and both visitors and staff have seen a thick, misty humanoid form. Electronic devices refuse to work and their batteries are drained of power. Near the mouth of the cave is a modern reconstruction of the Bell family cabin. The original, restored cabin is located near the Bellwood Cemetery, where the Bell family tombstones are located.

Bell Witch Cave and Bell Cabin are open May through October, Wednesday through Monday from 10:00 A.M. to 5:00 P.M. The site is closed on Tuesdays and the cave is closed when flooded. Admission fees apply.

CARNTON PLANTATION
1345 Carnton Lane
Franklin, TN 37064
(615) 794-0903
www.carnton.org

There was nothing really special about Carnton, Randal McGavock's plantation, until the last day of November 1864. There had been one tragic incident in which a farmhand had murdered one of the kitchen staff, but other than that, life was pretty normal on the big plantation. Then all the horrors of the Civil War came to Carnton. In one of the bloodiest encounters of the entire, blood-soaked conflict, the Second Battle of Franklin, ninety-five hundred men died or were wounded in a short five hours. McGavock's house was commandeered for use as a field hospital. According to Confederate records, when the house could hold no more men, the surrounding yard was filled with the wounded, dying, and dead. Among the fallen were four Southern generals. A few months after the battle, the McGavocks donated two acres of land for use as a cemetery, but by then the house was already filled with the residual energy of death and destruction.

The most frequently seen ghost at Carnton is that of Gen. Pat Cleburne, who paces across the back porch and checks the perimeter of the yard for Yankee infiltrators. On occasion, he has addressed the living, voicing grave concerns about the outcome of the battle and damning Gen. John Bell Hood for putting his men in such danger. Sometimes, in the late autumn, near the date of the battle, the sounds of screaming men, charging horses, and intense rifle and cannon fire can be heard on the grounds, along with a regimental band playing "Annie Laurie." There are several other Confederate soldiers here, too. One ghost paces back and forth on the front porch and others appear in and around the cemetery a few hundred yards away. There is also the murdered cook, who is heard making domestic sounds in the kitchen and whose disembodied head floats down the kitchen hall. A young woman in white is seen both in the second-floor hall and on the back porch, from which she occasionally floats across the adjoining garden area. Carnton has been a museum since 1977, and dozens of visitors and staff have experienced the ghosts both inside and outside the house.

Carnton Plantation is open April through December, Monday through Saturday from 9:00 A.M. to 4:00 P.M. and Sunday from 1:00 P.M. to 4:00 P.M. January through March it is open Monday through Friday from 9:00 A.M. to 4:00 P.M. It is closed on major holidays. The museum also hosts occasional ghost tours. Admission fees apply.

BELMONT MANSION
Belmont University Campus
1900 Belmont Boulevard
Nashville, TN 37212
(615) 460-5459
www.belmontmansion.com

Adelicia Hayes was a bright, kind, hard-working, and vivacious woman who endured more loss and grief in her life than most people can even imagine. In 1833, when Adelicia was sixteen, her fiancé died. A few years later, she married a much older man, Isaac Franklin, who died only seven years later, and none of their four children survived past the age of twelve. In 1849, she married for a second time. With her lawyer husband, John Acklen, she built the magnificent thirty-six-room villa they called Belmont, and while John saw to his law business, Adelicia singlehandedly ran the 8,400-acre plantation. Together they had six children, two of whom died of scarlet fever, only to be followed to the grave by their father, who was killed during the Civil War. Despite losing one fiancé, two husbands, and six children, Adelicia found the courage to marry again. She also found the time to open a college for girls, an institution that survived and grew into Belmont University, which now owns its founder's fine old plantation house.

Considering how hard Adelicia struggled to make her life work, it should come as no surprise that even in death she insists on keeping an eye on things at Belmont. Over the years, her fully formed apparition has been seen hundreds of times by visitors, staff, and security guards. Inevitably she is dressed in an antebellum hoop skirt and appears in nearly every room in her house. Her image is solid enough, or powerful enough, to set off alarms connected to motion detectors in the security system.

Belmont Mansion is open all year, Monday through Saturday from 10:00 A.M. to 4:00 P.M. and Sunday from 1:00 P.M. to 4:00 P.M. Groups larger than fifteen should call ahead. The mansion is closed on major holidays. Admission fees apply.

THE HERMITAGE
4580 Rachel's Lane
Nashville, TN 37076
(615) 889-2941
www.thehermitage.com

Andrew Jackson, the hero of the Battle of New Orleans and seventh president of the United States, owned the Hermitage plantation from 1804 until his death in 1845. During his busy career, he retreated here to relax from time to time. After he died, it took the state of Tennessee nearly forty years to declare the Hermitage an official historic site and begin much needed and long-overdue renovation work. By that time, Jackson's family no longer lived here, and the only two remaining caretakers refused to stay overnight because of the hauntings.

When the preservationists spent their first few nights at the Hermitage to take a complete survey of the house and chattels, they were awakened by the thundering sound of Old Hickory whipping his horse up the main staircase and down the second-floor hall. In the kitchen, some furious entity has spent decades creating an uproar with the sound of crashing pots and pans and smashing dishes, although no actual dishes or utensils are ever disturbed. From the front porch come the sounds of Jackson's slaves dragging their chains; apparitions of the slaves have been seen on the second-floor balcony leading to Jackson's bedroom. Why their spirits appear on Jackson's personal balcony is unknown. Now that the house has been restored to its former grandeur, Jackson no longer rides up and down the stairs, but the kitchen, porch, and balcony manifestations continue to occur from time to time.

The Hermitage is open daily April 1 through October 15 from 8:30 A.M. to 5:00 P.M. and October 16 through March 31 from 9:00 A.M. to 4:00 P.M. The site is closed Thanksgiving Day, Christmas Day, and the third week of January. Admission fees apply.

TEXAS

MISS MOLLY'S HOTEL
109 West Exchange Street
Fort Worth, TX 76106
(817) 626-1522
www.missmollyshotel.com

This 1910-era building has had several incarnations during its century-long life, but it has always been run for the convenience of those stopping by for a visit. When first constructed, it was a strait-laced boardinghouse called the Palace Rooms, where the live-in hostess and owner watched over her guests like a mother hen. By the 1920s, it had become the Oasis, a speakeasy, and during World War II, the once respectable boardinghouse had deteriorated into the Gayette Hotel, a sleazy brothel; both of these illegal businesses attracted enough violent undesirables to ensure the building would have the ghost-filled future that now marks Miss Molly's Hotel as one of the most active paranormal sites in all of Texas.

Nearly all eight guest rooms experience some type of haunting, and much of it seems to be associated with the sort of behavior you would expect from a lady of the evening. Male guests have felt fingers running through their hair and hands touching their thighs. In both hallways and rooms, the scent of old-fashioned perfume lingers. In a rare instance of ghosts actually making solid objects materialize out of thin air, half-century-old coins have magically appeared in unoccupied rooms. A wealth of other, more common manifestations include doors slamming open and closed, mysterious shadows moving across walls, lights inexplicably being turned on and off, toilets flushing by themselves, and glowing blue orbs appearing in Room 1.

There are at least two full-bodied apparitions here. One is the ghost of a girl of about eight or nine and the other is an attractive platinum blond from the 1940s who sometimes materializes on the edge of a startled guest's bed. Not surprisingly, Miss Molly's Hotel has been investigated numerous times by an array of ghost hunters, and every one of them has come away with a host of paranormal evidence, including photos and EVP recordings.

Miss Molly's Hotel is open all year. Although it is a bed-and-breakfast only, it is located directly above a full-service restaurant, the Fort Worth Star Café.

ASHTON VILLA
2328 Broadway
Galveston, TX 77550
(409) 762-3933
www.galvestonhistory.org/1859_Ashton_Villa.asp

James M. Brown made a fortune in railroading, banking, and the hardware business. With some of the profit, he built a truly Texas-sized mansion that he called Ashton Villa. When Brown started building his three-story house when the Civil War began in 1861, he was the richest man in Texas. He had a daughter named Betty, who was only six years old at the time. Because of its strategic importance, Galveston changed hands several times during the war, and the side that held sway made Ashton Villa their headquarters. Unlike most of the South, Galveston recovered quickly after the war, as did Jim Brown's fortune. For many years, Betty made her parents' home a base from which to live the life of a beautiful, spoiled brat. When her parents died, she remained in the grand house, filling it with souvenirs from her travels and festive lifestyle.

Betty eventually died and the house deteriorated. It was in danger of being lost until 1971, when it was rescued and restored. As so often happens, the revival of the house's physical and decorative structure brought about the revival of the dead, in this case the ghost of Betty Brown and at least one of her many male admirers. Betty's shockingly lifelike apparition spends most of its time on the grand stairway, in the upstairs hall, in a small room off the hall where she relaxed, and in the formal parlor known as the Gold Room. Although she always appears in formal dress, she has been reported to be one of the rare ghosts who actually changes clothes. In one memorable encounter with Betty, a night watchman was awakened by the sound of two people arguing. When he went into the Gold Room, he found Betty seated on the piano stool arguing with a tall, bearded man. Their heated exchange was heard clearly; the man was berating her for her frivolous life of partying and shallow vanity. After the man disappeared, Betty walked to her collections of fans which is on display, picked one up, looked into the mirror, and vanished, leaving the fan to fall to the floor. On other occasions, Betty has been known to give piano recitals, and the bedclothes in her old room rumple themselves no matter how often they are straightened out. Photos taken on the lawn often include Betty as an unexpected subject.

Ashton Villa closed after suffering severe damage during Hurricane Ike in September 2008. As of this writing, it is open for restoration-in-progress tours on Fridays and Saturdays at 2:00 P.M., 3:00 P.M., and 4:00 P.M.

CATFISH PLANTATION RESTAURANT
814 Water Street
Waxahachie, TX 75165
(972) 937-9468
www.catfishplantation.com

No one is quite sure when the ghosts first appeared in the Anderson house. It was probably sometime between 1970, when it was last used as a private home, and 1984, when it took on its current incarnation as the Catfish Plantation Restaurant. We do know that all three of the ghosts lived and died in the house. The oldest of the spirits is Elizabeth Anderson, whose father built the house in 1895. According to contemporary newspaper accounts, poor Elizabeth was murdered on her wedding day in 1920 by a jealous former boyfriend. Then there is a man known only as Will, who lived and died in the house during the depression years of the 1930s. Finally, there is Caroline, the last person to live in the house, who died there in 1970 at the age of eighty.

When the new owners took over the property in 1984, they were certain they were the only ones with a key. So who passed through locked doors to greet them with freshly brewed coffee and startle them by placing the big iced tea urn in the middle of the kitchen floor, stacking all the coffee cups neatly inside of it? It seems that this was the work of the unseen Caroline, who when in less friendly moods has been known to levitate cups, glasses, and various food items in front of startled employees and customers. Evidently, Caroline was a teetotaler, because the owners have virtually given up trying to keep their stock of wineglasses from being smashed.

Although Caroline is invisible, her two ghostly companions are not. The fully formed apparition of Will has been seen lounging on the front porch, but make no mistake, he is not as solid as he appears. Even when the local police approached him for loitering, he dematerialized in front of them. Elizabeth makes herself known in several ways. She sometimes announces her presence by the scent of roses. At other times, she materializes in the bay window in the front room. On at least one occasion, she wrote the name of a customer's child on a frosted window. Another time she followed a female patron home, where she awakened the woman in the middle of the night, appearing in full form from the waist up, saying a few kind words before vanishing.

Catfish Plantation Restaurant is open all year, Wednesday through Saturday from 11:00 A.M. to 9:00 P.M. and Sunday from 11:00 A.M. to 8:00 P.M.

VIRGINIA

BERKELEY PLANTATION
12602 Harrison Landing Road
Charles City, VA 23030
(804) 829-6018 or (888) 466-6018
www.berkeleyplantation.com

Virginia planter Benjamin Harrison III built this Federal-style mansion in 1726. In 1790, Benjamin Harrison VI received good advice on renovating the interior from fellow Virginian Thomas Jefferson. Between these two events, a fluke accident nearly wiped out the Harrison family. During a violent storm in 1744, William Harrison IV went to his children's bedroom to close the windows. Two daughters, one holding her infant brother, clustered around Harrison, when a bolt of lightning crashed through the glass killing everyone but the baby.

In 1773, future hero of the Battle of Tippecanoe and ninth president of the United States, William Henry Harrison, was born here. During the Civil War, the house was taken over by the Union for use as a hospital and headquarters for Gen. George B. McClellan. The surrounding property was used to quarter more than 140,000 Union troops. After the war the house slowly fell into disuse and disrepair, degenerating to the point that it was used as a cattle barn. At the dawn of the twentieth century the property was bought by John Jamieson, who had been stationed there as a drummer boy in 1862.

Jamieson brought the house back to life, and it was eventually opened to the public, but the many tragedies and deaths at the property left it very haunted. In the bedroom where three members of the Harrison family were killed by lightning, the ghost of a young girl has been seen standing near the window, which has been known to open and close by itself. The apparition of her father appears in the dining room and parlor, where he makes the glass in the chandelier shudder and tinkle. He also levitates fruit from the bowl on the dining room table, carries it around the room, and usually replaces it in the bowl. No one knows whose ghost is heard walking the wide planks of the attic floor. Outside the house the specters of a tall man in a Union uniform and a drummer boy are seen walking by the riverbank. The assumption is that they both died in the house when it was used as a hospital.

Berkeley Plantation is open daily from 9:30 A.M. to 4:30 P.M. It is closed on Thanksgiving and Christmas. Admission fees apply.

KENMORE PLANTATION
1201 Washington Avenue
Fredericksburg, VA 22401
(540) 373-3381
www.kenmore.org

The name of Fielding Lewis may not loom large in American history books, but as George Washington's brother-in-law, business partner, second cousin, and fellow revolutionary, his role in the founding of our country was considerable. Like Washington, Lewis was a planter, and he also ran a shipyard and store. Hardworking and thrifty, Lewis saved his money, married Washington's sister in 1750 at age twenty-five, and was cautious enough to wait twenty years before building the fine, expensive plantation house now known as Kenmore. During the Revolutionary War, Lewis served in the militia and earned the rank of colonel. He invested nearly his entire fortune in constructing an ammunition factory. The outflow of cash combined with the British blockade of American ports nearly put Lewis in bankruptcy; the stress and worry unquestionably hastened his death at fifty-six in December 1781, only two months after the British surrendered at Yorktown.

After Lewis's wife died in 1797, the plantation was sold and resold, its value, condition, and productivity constantly declining. In the Civil War, the house was used as a Union field hospital and it took heavy damage during the many battles fought in and around Fredericksburg. In 1880, the dilapidated mansion was renovated, but by 1920 it was again in danger of being bulldozed for new housing. Only then was it rescued, restored, and opened to the public. But the uncertain fate of his beleaguered businesses and home still weigh heavily on poor Fielding Lewis, because to this day he is often seen at his desk in a second-floor room, dressed in 1770s-era clothes, poring over his books and ledgers, a worried frown creasing his brow. Even when he is not visible, Lewis lets visitors know he is there; his heavy boots can be heard pacing back and forth in his study and the hall outside. On several occasions heavy fireplace andirons have mysteriously crashed to the floor.

Kenmore Plantation is open March through October from 10:00 A.M. to 5:00 P.M. and November through February from 10:00 A.M. to 4:00 P.M. It is closed Easter Sunday, Thanksgiving, Christmas Eve, Christmas Day, New Year's Eve, and New Year's Day. Entry fees apply.

GLENCOE INN
222 North Street
Portsmouth, VA 23704
(757) 397-8128
www.glencoeinn.com

Glencoe is an average-looking late Victorian house, and nothing spectacular or dreadful ever happened there. The most unusual aspect of this graceful old home may be its name, Glencoe, which its original owners gave to it in memory of one of the glens, or valleys, in their native Scotland. Like most houses that have survived more than a hundred years, it has changed hands numerous times and was poorly remodeled before it was rescued and renovated into a charming bed-and-breakfast inn. One part of the house that had survived the years was its old-fashioned rose garden, but the disruption and havoc of the restoration process demanded that it be largely replaced and restored.

Somewhere between the restoration of the house and the disruption of the rose garden, one of the house's former owners seems to have been resurrected. The current owners theorize that she probably lived there during the 1920s, because wallpaper from that era was printed with a delicate rose pattern and her dress is also reminiscent of the period. She appears today as a woman in her mid-eighties and only materializes in the restored rose garden. Sometimes she putters among the flowers and at other times she stares into the distance, seeing a world long gone but still fresh in her memory. During the winter, when even ghosts know they can't work in the garden, she still manages to make her presence known. In the entry hall of the old house, even during the coldest months, guests sometimes catch the delicate scent of freshly cut roses.

Glencoe Inn is open all year.

ADAM THOROUGHGOOD HOUSE
1636 Parish Road
Virginia Beach, VA 23455
(757) 460-7588 or (757) 431-4000
http://virginiabeachhistory.org/thoroughgoodhouse.html

Adam Thoroughgood never saw the house that now bears his name. Born in the village of Kings Lynn in County Norfolk, England, around 1605, he wanted desperately to come to the American colonies, but had no money to pay for his passage. Indenturing himself to a colonial master, Thoroughgood finally came to America in 1622. He worked long enough to repay the cost of his ticket plus interest, as well as the cost of his room and board, and he set up his own tobacco farm in 1635. He became a leader in his tiny community, was elected to Virginia's House of Burgesses, and helped found the town of Norfolk. He did all this before his death at age thirty-six. His land and the small wooden cottage he lived in eventually passed to his grandson, who built the current house around 1680.

Looking more like something from Renaissance England than colonial America, it is a simple brick house with two rooms on each of its two floors. It is also the oldest brick structure in America. How it survived more than three-and-a-quarter centuries is a miracle in itself, particularly since almost none of its history between 1680 and 1957 was ever recorded. In 1957, the house was restored with funds from the city of Norfolk and the Chrysler Museum, but by the late 1980s, Norfolk and Virginia Beach were squabbling over the property that straddled their mutual boundary. The house and grounds were officially turned over to Virginia Beach in 2003 and yet another restoration got underway. Because so much of the house's history has been lost, no one knows whether the ghosts of Thoroughgood's grandson and his wife returned to the property during one of the relatively recent restorations or whether they have been there for more than three centuries. In either case, a female entity has been seen carrying a lighted candle around the house's interior and a man in a suit of brown, coarse-woven fabric has been seen in the hallway and rooms by staff and visitors alike.

Adam Thoroughgood House is open all year, Tuesday through Saturday from 10:00 A.M. to 5:00 P.M. and Sunday from 1:00 P.M. to 5:00 P.M. The last tour begins at 4:30 P.M. daily. It is closed on Mondays and major holidays. Entry fees apply.

PEYTON RANDOLPH HOUSE
Colonial Williamsburg
P.O. Box 1776
Williamsburg, VA 23187
(757) 229-1000
www.history.org

If the passage of time, tragedy, and renovation all contribute to the likelihood of spirit manifestation, there are few places in the country more likely to have ghosts than Colonial Williamsburg. One of the two most haunted places here is the Randolph House, which was built in 1715 by Sir John Randolph and later inherited by his son Peyton. In 1824, the house was sold to Mary Monroe

Peachy, whose life seemed to attract tragedy. Already a widow, Mary suffered the deaths of several of her children, one by falling from a tree and others from various sicknesses that were incurable at the time. Adding to her miserable life, a relative committed suicide in the drawing room of the house and a young, retired Civil War soldier who was renting a room contracted tuberculosis and died there.

Although apparitions have been reported in the house for more than two hundred years, only one of them seems to match the description of any of the individuals who died there. The spirit most likely to be identified is that of an elderly woman wearing a long nightgown and a lace nightcap who appears in a small, oak-paneled bedroom on the second floor. Believed to be Mary herself, the ghost has been known to address people by name before wringing her hands, weeping, and moaning like someone in mourning. Most disturbingly, the figure is translucent; her skull is visible through the ghostly flesh of her face. Several female employees and guests have encountered a formless, malignant entity on the second-floor landing who has tried to push them down the stairs; consequently, many female park employees refuse to work in the house. People report hearing groans in the basement and one male employee was locked in the basement by unseen hands. Numerous staff and guests have encountered a man in colonial blues and found him so lifelike that they tried to talk to him, only to have him vanish before their eyes. There are also numerous reports of the sound of a mirror shattering and of heavy military boots walking across the wood floors.

Colonial Williamsburg is open 365 days a year from 9:00 A.M. to 5:00 P.M. Some evening events, such as lantern-light tours, are available. Check the Web site or call for upcoming events. Entry fees apply.

GEORGE WYTHE HOUSE
Colonial Williamsburg
P.O. Box 1776
Williamsburg, VA 23187
(757) 229-1000
www.history.org

George Wythe was an outstanding man. As America's first law professor, he taught and later advised Thomas Jefferson. As a member of the Continental Congress, he became a signer of the Declaration of Independence. His house is one of only five original structures at Colonial Williamsburg and has been standing on tree-lined Gloucester Street since it was built in 1755.

As is true with the Randolph house, we don't know who the ghosts are in this house. One is a woman whose high-heeled shoes are heard going up the stairs, and she is assumed to be the same entity occasionally seen emerging from or disappearing into a bedroom closet wearing a satin gown and red shoes. The same figure has been seen standing on the staircase and sometimes appears so lifelike that guests and guides have spoken to her, only to have her melt away into thin air. This ghost is believed to be Ann Skipworth, a friend of the Wythe family. An unidentified group of men in eighteenth-century clothing has been seen lounging in the wingback chairs in the study. Outside the library, a frowning man from the same period paces up and down the hallway. Unseen ghosts include a couple who argues in the parlor and a woman whose old-fashioned floral perfume can sometimes be detected near the back of the hallway. Visitors experience cold spots on the second-floor landing, even on the hottest days, and the sound of phantom furniture is heard being moved around on the main floor. This wide and varied collection of phenomena leads us to believe that this house is a ghost magnet and may draw entities from other sites that exist, or once existed, in and around Williamsburg.

Colonial Williamsburg is open 365 days a year from 9:00 A.M. to 5:00 P.M. Some evening events, such as lantern-light tours, are available. Check the Web site or call for upcoming events. Entry fees apply.

There are several ghost tours of Colonial Williamsburg, including The Ghosts of Williamsburg, (877) 624-4678, www.theghosttour .com; and Williamsburg Ghost Lantern Tours, (757) 897-9600, www.williamsburgprivatetours.com/ghost.htm.

MOORE HOUSE
Yorktown Battlefield
Colonial National Historical Park
106 Hamilton Road
P.O. Box 210
Yorktown, VA 23690
(757) 898-2410
http://www.nps.gov/york/historyculture/moore-house.htm

Augustine Moore bought this house and five hundred acres of land from his brother-in-law in 1760. Already a successful merchant, Moore did not work the land himself but lived the life of a gentleman farmer, leasing out farming rights to others including his son, Augustine Jr. During the Revolutionary War, several battles came perilously close to the Moore property, and during one of these, Augustine Jr. was struck and killed by a stray bullet. In October 1781, only days before the British surrendered to Continental forces led by Gen. George Washington, Moore's neighbor, John Turner, crept close enough to watch the battle, and he too was hit by a stray bullet and died in his wife's arms. Only days after Turner's death, in the parlor of the Moore House, British general Lord Charles Cornwallis signed the surrender papers ending the Revolutionary War.

After the deaths of Augustine and Lucy Moore at the end of the eighteenth century, the house passed through many hands and was again swept into the midst of death and destruction during the 1862 Peninsula Campaign of the Civil War. The owners fled the battle zone but the house suffered heavy shell damage and the owners chose not to return. The house was rescued from neglect and abandonment in 1881, when it was repaired and opened to the public for the one hundredth anniversary of Cornwallis's surrender. In 1931, the property was turned over to the National Park

Service, which restored it to its 1780s appearance and apparently awakened one or more ghosts in the process. The unidentified spirits seem to be a fairly lazy lot; the only evidence of their existence is the continual rumpling of almost every bed in the second-floor bedrooms.

Yorktown Battlefield Park is open daily from 9:00 A.M. to sunset. It is closed on Thanksgiving, Christmas, and New Year's Day. The Moore House is open as staffing permits; please check with the park service for dates and times. Entry fees apply. The same entry fee for the Moore House will permit entrance to the Nelson House as well.

NELSON HOUSE
508 Main Street
Yorktown, VA 23690
(757) 898-2410
www.nps.gov/york/historyculture/nelson-house.htm

If this grand old townhouse was famous for nothing else, it would be noteworthy because during the nearly 250 years it served as a private residence, only two families lived there. The house was constructed in 1730 by Thomas "Scotch Tom" Nelson, who arrived in America in 1705 and built a substantial business as a merchant. His grandson, Thomas Nelson Jr., was a member of the Continental Congress, a signer of the Declaration of Independence, governor of Virginia, and a brigadier general during the Battle of Yorktown. While Nelson was fighting, the British commander Gen. Lord Charles Cornwallis set up headquarters in the Nelson House. The Nelson family was still in the house during the Civil War, when it was alternately commandeered for use as a Confederate, and later Union, hospital; the death toll taken here is beyond contemplating. In 1914, the Nelson family sold their grand old house to Captain and Mrs. George P. Blow, whose family remained in the house for three generations until 1968, when it was purchased by the National Park Service and restored to its original appearance.

As is the case in many venerable old houses that have witnessed war and destruction, the Nelson House spirits are difficult to identify. The two most frequently seen are a young man dressed in a red British uniform who appears now and then throughout the house and a weeping woman who is confined to the third floor but can be witnessed inside the house and peering through the attic windows at passersby. The weeping woman also produces orbs of light that have been photographed inside and outside the third floor. A number of other entities seem to come and go. There have been reports of ghosts dressed in costumes ranging from the mid-1700s through the mid-1900s, but most of these spirits are either transient or have been reported only on a few occasions. The house also manifests cold spots, phantom footsteps, and inexplicable flickering lights.

The Nelson House is located in Yorktown itself, but it is part of the Yorktown Battlefield National Park. It is open as staffing permits, so check with the park service for dates and times. Entry fees apply. The same fee will also permit entrance to the Moore House.

WEST VIRGINIA

FEDERAL ARSENAL GUEST HOUSE

Harpers Ferry National Historical Park
P.O. Box 65
Harpers Ferry, WV 25425
(304) 535-6029
www.nps.gov/hafe

The village of Harpers Ferry has a long and eventful history. Much of that is because of the town's strategic location sixty miles northwest of Washington, D.C., where it sits at the confluence of the Potomac and Shenandoah rivers. The area's first brush with fame and disaster came in 1859, when abolitionist John Brown and eighteen compatriots raided the federal arsenal there in hopes of igniting a slave rebellion. United States marines eventually suppressed the uprising, but seventeen people, including troops, local civilians, and some of Brown's men, were killed. Several surviving raiders, including Brown, were later hanged.

The trouble only got worse when the town changed hands five times during the Civil War, with each reversal of fortune costing hundreds of military and civilian lives. In the wake of death and destruction came repeated cholera epidemics, and only a few years after the war, a flood nearly wiped out the town. Thanks to this litany of death, Harpers Ferry has become one of the most haunted towns in America—and its most haunted building is the guest house at the old federal arsenal.

No one knows who these ghosts are or why they are here. The one most often seen is the fully formed apparition of a scowling man in full nineteenth-century dress, including a brocade vest, top hat, and walking stick. He appears at the top of the servants staircase. At least one staff member insists this spirit tried to push her down the stairs. Then there is the image of a woman wearing a gray Victorian dress and a hooded cloak who is accompanied by a child about eight years old. The ghostly pair appears on the staircase but does not move, vanishing within seconds. In the front room there have also been reports of the figure of a workman in nineteenth-century clothes carrying the body of a dead man. If you happen to wander down the streets of Harpers Ferry near the old firehouse, look for the tall, gaunt man with wild white hair and a beard. He may smile and even agree to let you take his picture, but his image never shows up on the print; he is John Brown, executed more than 150 years ago.

Harpers Ferry National Historical Park is open daily from 8:00 A.M. to 5:00 P.M. and is closed on Thanksgiving, Christmas, and New Year's Day. There is no entry fee, but there is a parking fee.

BLENNERHASSETT MANSION
Blennerhassett Island Historical State Park
137 Juliana Street
Parkersburg, WV 26101
(304) 420-4800 or (800) 225-5982
www.blennerhassettislandstatepark.com

Harman Blennerhassett had every opportunity and advantage, but he seemed determined to ruin himself and those around him. While still living in his native Ireland in 1796, he courted and married his niece Margaret. Ostracized by their scandalized family, the Blennerhassetts fled to the frontiers of the United States, where Harman purchased an island on the Ohio River. Two years later, he constructed a magnificent, seven-thousand-square-foot Palladian mansion, filling it with the finest furniture from London and Paris. Only seven years later, in 1805, Blennerhassett became involved in a plot hatched by former vice president Aaron Burr (who had killed Alexander Hamilton in a duel the previous year) to seize the entire Louisiana Territory and establish a new country. Word of the plot reached President Thomas Jefferson, who sent the Virginia militia to plunder the island and arrest the men involved. Blennerhassett was eventually freed, but his family was ruined and had to leave the island. In 1811, only four years after their hasty retreat, the mansion burned to the ground.

By 1976, Blennerhassett Island had become a state park, and the massive project of reconstructing the long-gone mansion was initiated. The work resurrected the ghost of Margaret and two of her children who died on the island during the family's short occupancy. Margaret, both alone and in the company of her children, is seen walking near the shore and around the exterior of house. On one occasion, she has been caught on videotape coming up the house's cellar steps. Another ghost on the island probably predates the Blennerhasset occupancy. He is a Native American who has been seen tracking game in the woods for centuries. He is only spotted from behind and any attempt to approach him causes him to vanish.

Blennerhassett Island Historical State Park is open May through October. The house is open Tuesday through Friday from 11:00 A.M. to 4:30 P.M., Saturday from 11:00 A.M. to 5:30 P.M., and Sunday from 12:00 P.M. to 5:30 P.M. The house is closed on Mondays and November through April. Entry fees apply. Parkersburg offers a ghost tour. Call (304) 428-7978 or visit http://users.wirefire.com/magick.

BOREMAN WHEEL HOUSE RESTAURANT
406 Avery Street
Parkersburg, WV 26101
(304) 485-3838

Arthur Boreman built this house for his daughter while he was serving as West Virginia's first governor during the Civil War. Convenient for the family, the house was located directly across the street from the Boremans' house, but rather awkwardly, it was also situated right next to a military hospital where thousands of wounded Union soldiers were brought and many of them died.

Ghost hunters who have investigated the house, which has long been a popular bar and restaurant, believe many of the ghosts may have migrated from the old hospital at some point in time, possibly during the renovation process. In the basement, a ghostly bartender has been seen standing behind the bar where he smiles at visitors, says "Hello," and disappears. Elsewhere in the building, customers and staff have heard whispering phantom voices and the sounds of footsteps walking across wood floors. Glasses fall from their shelves without reason, and in the attic, glowing orbs have been photographed.

Boreman Wheel House is open all year for lunch, dinner, and drinks, Monday through Saturday. On weekends they have live music.

Parkersburg offers a ghost tour. Call (304) 428-7978 or visit http://users.wirefire.com/magick.

MIDWEST

ILLINOIS

BEVERLY UNITARIAN CHURCH
10244 S. Longwood Drive
Chicago, IL 60643
(773) 233-7080
www.beverlyunitarian.org

In 1886, real estate promoter and novelist Robert Givens built a new house in what was then Chicago's most expensive neighborhood. Not content with houses like those of his neighbors, Givens built a castle to remind him of the medieval ruins in his native Ireland. Because there is a limited market for used castles, the gigantic house, by then known as Irish Castle, went through many hands after Givens died. It was a doctor's office, then a girls school, and finally in 1942 the home of the Beverly Unitarian Church.

The ghost that haunts the church is thought to have been a student at the Chicago Female College, which owned the building in the 1930s. Evidently the girl died of influenza, not uncommon in the days before effective treatments, and since then her spirit has continued to live here. The first sighting took place in the 1960s, when a church custodian encountered a young girl who insisted the place had changed since she lived there. The custodian was understandably confused; no one had lived there in more than twenty years. Since that first encounter, the young girl has popped up frequently enough that many members of the congregation, all of the pastors, and numerous guests have seen her as a fully formed entity. On other occasions, she manifests herself as a tinkling sound that seems to come from everywhere at once. Sometimes she appears only as a candleflame moving from window to window and up the staircase.

Beverly Unitarian Church rents out the church hall for meetings and special functions. Please respect the fact that this is a house of worship.

GLESSNER HOUSE MUSEUM
1800 S. Prairie Avenue
Chicago, IL 60616
(312) 326-1480
http://glessnerhouse.org

Born and raised in Chicago, Henry Hobson Richardson went on to become one of America's best known architects of the late nineteenth century, and this is as much his story as it is the story of J. J. Glessner and his wonderful house. Glessner had made his fortune in farm machinery, and when it came time to build his own house on Chicago's trendy Prairie Avenue, he called on Richardson to design the structure. Richardson's architectural style, identified by its use of medieval castle-like appearances, stone construction, and arched doors and windows, had already made him both rich and famous. Despite the fact that he was only forty-eight years old, Richardson knew he was dying. The Glessner House would be his last and greatest achievement. Richardson never saw the house completed, but the Glessners lived there for nearly fifty years, and that whole time, they kept a portrait of Richardson in their house.

It seems that Richardson himself was also there. He just couldn't bear to leave his last project behind. When John Glessner died in 1936, the house deteriorated and was only saved from demolition thirty years later when a group of citizens raised the funds to buy and restore the property. Now open to the public as a museum, everyone can share Richardson's last project, along with his ghost, just like the Glessners did. A moving cold spot wanders through the rooms and halls, and a white apparition is often seen on the stairs and in the master bedroom. If you happen to visit the Glessner House and meet a heavyset, bearded man who delights in telling you all about the architecture, the design, and the symmetry of the house, don't be too surprised and don't bother to ask the staff if he works there. They will already know that you, like others before, have had an encounter with the ghost of Henry Hobson Richardson.

Glessner House Museum is open Wednesday through Sunday. Tours are conducted at 1:00 P.M. and 3:00 P.M. Group tours are avail-

able for ten or more by appointment with four weeks' notice. Entry fees apply except on Wednesday, when tours are free.

CULVER HOUSE
412 Prairie Avenue
Decatur, IL 62521
(312) 922-1742

The old Culver House is now a sad shadow of its former glorious self, but maybe there are good reasons. Construction on this grand Romanesque-style mansion began in 1881 on land that had once been a Native American burial ground. While there is no evidence that the original builder knew about this beforehand, records show that workmen uncovered numerous human bones during excavation work. Whether this was part of the reason why Josiah Clokey stopped construction on his house is unknown, but the partially finished project was purchased and completed by John Culver.

The Culvers had no more than settled in to their new house when one evening, as they were seated around the dining room table, something very large and frightening swooped down the dining room chimney, terrifying the family. Culver bricked up the dining room fireplace and the family evidently experienced no more living nightmares. After Culver's death in 1943, the house stood empty, but passersby reported seeing a man standing in the first-floor window. Eventually the house was turned into an apartment building, but odd and unsettling things began to happen. In the 1960s, one resident committed suicide, the house caught fire and nearly burned down, and in 1988, a resident was murdered. Shortly thereafter the old Culver house was abandoned. The house has been purchased by a preservation foundation and is slated to be restored, but as of this writing it still stands empty and forlorn.

Culver House is abandoned and condemned as of this writing. Entry to the property is strictly forbidden.

OLD SLAVE HOUSE MUSEUM
State Highway 13
Junction, IL 62954

John H. Crenshaw made his fortune in the 1830s by mining and refining salt, but because salt mining is horrible work, he had difficulty finding employees for his mines and refinery. Although Illinois law prohibited slavery, Crenshaw discovered a loophole that allowed for leasing slaves from Southern owners. He hated having to pay for their use, however, so he hired thugs to kidnap free black men and women who were then forced to work in the mines and refinery. Sequestering his captives in the attic of his Hickory Hill house, he kept them chained and shackled every minute they were not working. An added bonus came in the form of nearly three hundred infants who were born to his captive women and who Crenshaw raised until they were old enough to be smuggled to the South and sold. In 1842, Crenshaw was arrested on charges of slave trading. His money and power guaranteed that he was never sent to prison, and the full extent of Crenshaw's crimes did not come to light until after he sold the house in the mid-1860s. By then it was massively haunted by the spirits of those he had held in captivity.

In the 1920s, Hickory Hill was opened as a private museum, and from the start, visitors reported frightening experiences in the attic. As they climbed the stairs, guests were overcome with feelings of anxiety and dread and reported screams, moans, whimpers, and the sounds of dozens of unintelligible, mumbling voices emanating from the attic walls. At least 150 people have attempted to spend the night in the attic. The first was an exorcist named Hickman Wittington, who died only hours later. Every investigator since then has run terrified from the house within a matter of minutes. By 1996, the house had deteriorated to the point that it had to be closed, but in 2000 it was purchased by the state of Illinois, which plans to restore it and reopen it as a museum. Now called the Old Slave House Museum, it was still closed as of the date of this book's publication.

Old Slave House Museum is currently closed. Entry to the property is strictly forbidden as of this writing, and the site is heavily patrolled. You can check on the progress of the restoration by visiting the Web site of the Illinois State Historic Preservation Agency at www.illinoishistory.gov or by calling them at (217) 758-1511.

VOORHIES CASTLE
State Highway 105
Bement, IL 61813
(888) 452-6474
www.voorhiescastle.com

Voorhies Castle was only ever a castle in name, but Voorhies used to be a real town. Now the location is virtually abandoned and the castle is nothing more than a tourist attraction. The turreted, Shingle-style house was built in 1890 by Nels Larson, a Swedish immigrant who had amassed a small fortune in land, tenant farms, and businesses near Bement. By all accounts, Nels was a hard taskmaster, but he was devoted to his wife Johannah and at least civil to their children. As is so often the case, when things went bad for Nels, they all fell apart at once. In 1914, Johannah was found crumpled at the bottom of the stairs where she had died of an apparent heart attack. Stunned, Nels left the house and never returned, leaving everything just as it was at the moment of her death. After Nels died in 1921, the Larson children rented out the house, but no one would stay for long and it slowly deteriorated.

It seems no one wanted to live there because of the odd happenings. Lights turned on and off by themselves, locked windows opened on their own, the sound of footsteps was heard on the stairs, off-key piano notes played in the distance, and glowing orbs shot through the house with wild abandon. In the east tower, a shadowy figure, thought to be Johannah, appears at the window. Battery-powered equipment refuses to work. Mediums and psychics that have visited Voorhies Castle nearly all refuse to stay more than a few minutes. The house has been restored and is open to the public. It is listed in the National Register of Historic Places.

Voorhies Castle is open by appointment to groups of ten or more. Entry fees apply.

INDIANA

OLD SHERIFF'S HOUSE AND JAIL

226 S. Main Street
Crown Point, IN 46307
(219) 633-3536
www.lakenetnwi.net/member/oldsheriffshouse

Back in 1882, the good citizens of Crown Point collected a fund to construct a house for their local county sheriffs to use while in office. The completed structure was a sturdy Second Empire house with an imposing mansard roof and lots of space for the sheriff's family and offices. In 1926, the town added a fine new two-story jail to the back of the house, so that the sheriff and his men had easy access to their prisoners. Nothing much ever happened in Crown Point or the surrounding Lake County area except for the time in 1934 when the notorious John Dillinger was held in the jail while awaiting trial for murder. Dillinger used a razor blade to carve a pistol from a block of wood, dyed it black with shoe polish, and bluffed his way out of jail, making his escape. Not that it did Dillinger much good. The very next Sunday, he was gunned down outside Chicago's Biograph Theatre by G-man Melvin Purvis and his deputies.

The sheriff's house and jail remained in use until 1958, when a new jail replaced the old one and the sheriffs began commuting from their own homes. No one knows the identity of the ghosts that haunt the old jail, but they have been photographed staring out through the bared windows and walking around the hall near the cells. Numerous visitors have been treated to the eerie sight of heavy cell doors opening and closing on their own and the sounds of bars rattling, footsteps, and distant voices.

Old Sheriff's House and Jail was still undergoing restoration as of this writing, but portions were already open to the public. Tours are available on Saturday mornings, June through September at 9:00 A.M. to 11:30 A.M. Entry fees apply.

HANNAH HOUSE

3801 Madison Avenue
Indianapolis, IN 46227
(317) 787-8486
www.thehannahmansion.org

Sometimes the best intentions in the world are not enough to save a family or a house from tragedy. Such is the case of the Hannah House. Alexander Hannah, who built his twenty-four-room Italianate mansion in 1858, was an honest, upright man. He was a member of the Indiana state legislature and offered his house as a stop on the Underground Railroad, helping fugitive slaves escape to Canada. One night one of the freed slaves staying in Hannah's basement accidentally kicked over an oil lamp. In seconds the room became an inferno, killing everyone inside. Because aiding runaway slaves was illegal, Hannah had the bodies interred in the basement of his home. Sometime later, his wife Elizabeth became pregnant, but what should have been a happy time turned to tragedy when the child died in the womb and had to be surgically extracted.

The Hannah House changed hands several times over the decades, but ghostly activity was only reported in 1967 when Alexander Hannah, dressed in his long black frock coat and sporting muttonchop whiskers, appeared on the second-floor landing. Since then the house has experienced hundreds of paranormal events. The room in which Elizabeth lost her child sometimes stinks of rotting flesh and at other times it smells of roses; the door opens and closes even when locked. Hannah continues to appear on the landing and balcony, and the spirit of an elderly woman is seen upstairs where whispering voices are heard, cold spots move from room to room, and footfalls go up and down the stairs. On the main floor, a chandelier has been filmed swinging by itself and kitchen utensils have flown across the room. In the basement, phantom slaves have been seen huddling in a corner and the sounds of smashing glass, moans, and scratching noises are frequently heard. The staff of the Hannah House is justly proud of their spirits.

Hannah House is usually open from 1:00 P.M. to 4:00 P.M. Dates vary, so visit their Web site or call for information. Hannah House also hosts the Hannah House Experience, an all-night ghost hunt teaming professionals with visitors. These events last from 8:00 P.M. to 4:00 A.M. and tend to sell out six months in advance. Fees apply to tours and events.

HACIENDA MEXICAN RESTAURANT
700 Lincoln Way West
Mishawaka, IN 46544
(574) 259-8541 or (800) 541-3227
www.haciendafiesta.com

What is now the Hacienda Mexican Restaurant was once a fine old Victorian home. We have been unable to discover the names of the house's original owners, the exact date of the tragedy, or the names of the victims, but according to employees past and present, as well as numerous customers, some odd things happen here. According to the story, a previous owner had an affair with his maid. When she became pregnant, shame drove the owner to shoot himself in the basement and the maid hanged herself on the second floor.

For at least as long as the house has been operating as a restaurant, fleeting apparitions have been seen throughout the building, along with the sound of whispered voices and moans heard near the attic door. One recurring voice clearly says, "Job's done, go home now." Lights go on and off by themselves, including those in what are now the restrooms. Faucets turn on and off by themselves. Manifestations in the room that used to be the restaurant's second-floor office, and possibly where the distraught maid ended her life, are so intense that the room is no longer used.

Hacienda Mexican Restaurant is open for lunch and dinner all week throughout the year. It is closed on Christmas Day.

IOWA

BRUCEMORE

2160 Linden Drive SE
Cedar Rapids, IA 52403
(319) 362-7375
www.brucemore.org

The lovely old Queen Anne-style mansion now known as Brucemore is interesting for more reasons than the ghosts that inhabit its library. In 1886, Caroline Sinclair had been widowed for five years and was struggling to raise her six children in a house that was too small. With the hefty inheritance left to her by her late husband, Thomas, she commissioned the construction of a house she called Fairhome. By the dawn of the new century, Caroline's children had grown up and left, so she swapped houses with George Bruce Douglas and his wife, Irene. In 1905, the Douglases and their three children moved into the house, undertook major renovations, and renamed the house Brucemore. Ownership of the mansion remained in the Douglas family until 1981, when it was deeded to the National Trust for Historic Preservation, which now operates the home as a museum.

Around the time of the 1905 renovation work, an unknown spirit in the house apparently became active, but limited its manifestations to the library. George Douglas called in a professor from the University of Chicago who had an interest in the then-popular realm of spiritualism. Douglas refused, however, to allow the man to carry out extensive investigations for fear of unwanted publicity. From 1905 until the present, the invisible ghost in the library has been laughing, groaning, and moving objects around on a regular basis. From time to time, a glowing shape has also been seen in this room. While most entities are confined to limited areas, it is rare that only one room in a house is haunted, at least to this extent.

Brucemore is open from March through December, Tuesday through Saturday from 10:00 A.M. to 3:00 P.M., and on Sunday from 12:00 P.M. to 3:00 P.M. It is closed on all major holidays. Entry fees apply. Discounts are available for groups of twenty or more with advance reservations.

MATHIAS HAM HOUSE
2241 Lincoln Avenue
Dubuque, IA 52001
(563) 557-9545
www.mississippirivermuseum.com/features_historicsites_ham.cfm

Mathias Ham started out small. In 1837, he had a few packet boats on the Mississippi River and a two-story, five-room house on a bluff overlooking the river. In 1856, Ham's first wife died, but most of his children were grown, so he remarried and completely rebuilt his house for his new wife. The new house was a mighty thing with twenty-three rooms, a grand staircase, and a massive cupola that nearly covered the roof. Mathias Ham eventually lost most of his money in real estate speculation and then died. Soon after, his wife also died.

After many of their children died, one daughter, Sarah, remained alone in the grand old mansion. One night during the 1890s, Sarah heard someone break into her house, but the intruder left without bothering her or doing any damage. The next day, she alerted her neighbors to the incident, telling them that if it happened again she would set a lamp in her bedroom window so they knew she needed help. It did happen again, but plucky Sarah didn't need any help. By the time the neighbors got there, Sarah had shot twice through her bedroom door and all that was left of the intruder was a trail of blood leading down the stairs, out the door, and toward the river.

By 1964, the Ham House had become a museum. At least one ghost, and possibly two, still lives there. Late at night a light is seen moving through the house's darkened hallways and a general ill-at-ease feeling permeates the house. Footsteps and other odd noises are frequently heard in the second-floor hall, shuffling noises are heard in the basement, and securely locked windows unlock and open by themselves. On one occasion, the old pump organ played by itself even though the bellows were rotted away and it had not worked in many years.

Mathias Ham House is open May through September, seven days a week, from 10:00 A.M. to 5:00 P.M. The last tour of the day begins at 4:00 P.M. Entry fees apply. Group rates are available.

VILLISCA AX MURDER HOUSE
323 East 4th Street
Villisca, IA 50864
(712) 621-4291
www.villiscaiowa.com

Once upon a time Villisca, Iowa, was like most towns of Middle America—small, neat, quiet, and friendly. But all that changed on the night of June 9, 1912, when J. B. Moore, his wife Sarah, their four children, and two of their children's friends were hacked to death by an unknown assailant after returning home from a church social. In spite of an intense manhunt, a string of suspects, and even a few arrests, the murderer was never caught and the case remains unsolved. Ever since that day, the Moore house has been known as the Villisca Ax Murder House and has played host to a continuing series of eerie, unexplained phenomena.

The hauntings were first reported in 1931. They have died down for decades at a time, but increased dramatically after the house was restored to its 1912 appearance and opened as a museum in 1994. An ax-wielding phantom has been seen in Sarah and J. B.'s bedroom, the voices of phantom children have been heard and recorded, glowing orbs have been photographed, and tours have been interrupted by moving objects, falling lamps, and terrifying banging noises. Dozens of amateur and professional ghost hunters and psychics have confirmed that the old house is one very haunted place. The house is listed in the National Register of Historic Places, and a display on the murders of the Moore family can be seen in the local library.

Villisca Ax Murder House is open for tours from April through November from 9:00 A.M. to 4:00 P.M. Entry fees apply. Discounts are available for large groups and school tours. Tours last from one to two hours.

KANSAS

TUCK U INN AT GLICK MANSION
503 N. Second Street
Atchison, KS 66002
(913) 367-9110 or (866) 367-8101
www.glickmansion.com

When George Glick began work on his mansion in 1873, he was already a Civil War veteran, lawyer, and Kansas legislator. By 1879, he had been elected governor of Kansas and undertaken a major expansion of his house. Over the years, the work continued, and in 1909, two years prior to his death, Glick deeded the property to his daughter Jennie and her husband, James Orr. The Orrs again set to work completely revamping the house, altering it from its mid-Victorian appearance to a more modern Tudor Revival style. By 1944, both of the Orrs had died and the house passed through several hands before being transformed into the Tuck U Inn in the 1980s.

No one is quite sure when the hauntings began, or who the entities are, but throughout the house strange sounds are heard at night, disembodied footsteps are heard at all hours and doors open and close by themselves.

Tuck U Inn at Glick Mansion is open all year. Atchison also offers a ghost tour. For information, call (800) 234-1854 or visit www.atchisonkansas.net/v_haunted.htm.

BROWN MANSION
2019 S. Walnut Street
Coffeyville, KS 67337
(800) 626-3357
www.kansastravel.org/brownmansion.htm

Most people who have heard of Coffeyville only relate it to the last, abortive raid of the notorious Dalton Gang, carried out in 1892. But Coffeyville has another interesting bit of history, the Brown Mansion. Three stories in height, surrounded by verandas, and replete with a bowling alley and ballroom, it was and is the showplace of the town.

By the time William and Nancy Brown completed work on their home in 1906, they had already lost three infant children. The surviving children then were their daughter Violet, who was nineteen and already wed, and their son Donald, who was seven. Donald joined his three brothers in death at the age of eleven in 1911. Alone in the big house, William and Nancy locked Donald's room and never reopened it. By the 1930s, the two were elderly, so Violet moved home to care for them and continued living there after their deaths. In 1970, Violet sold her family home to the local historical society, removing only those things she would need at the nursing home. But the Coffeyville Historical Society inherited more than a grand house, complete with all of its furnishings and bric-a-brac.

Locals report that at night glowing green lights flit across the mansion's grounds, but inside the house the hauntings are far more numerous and intense. In the third-floor ballroom visitors hear the sound of a child running or the laughter of long-departed guests. Some people catch the scent of William's cherry-blend tobacco. He has been spotted in his smoking jacket in the second-floor hall and on the main floor. A woman, probably Nancy, has been photographed on the stairs and furnishings have apparently moved from place to place. In the basement, the sound of rolling bowling balls and the crash of pins can be heard, and in the butler's old room, the bed is frequently mussed up. Although the management of the Brown Mansion refuses to talk about it, there is little doubt that the Browns have remained here long after death.

Brown Mansion is open May through October, Thursday through Monday from 11:00 A.M. to 4:00 P.M. The last tour of the day begins at 3:00 P.M. In March, April, November, and December, the house is open Saturday and Sunday only from 11:00 A.M. to 4:00 P.M. Entry fees apply.

SAUER CASTLE
935 Shawnee Road
Kansas City, KS 66103

Today the Sauer Castle looks like something out of a bad horror movie, but in its heyday it was a stunning example of German Gothic Revival architecture. When Anton Sauer moved west from New York in 1868, he was a widower with five children searching for a new life and a cure for his tuberculosis. Shortly after moving to Kansas City, he met and married his second wife, Mary, who was a widow with two children of her own. Needing a place large enough for their brood (which would eventually include five more children), Sauer bought and renovated the house now known as Sauer's Castle. By the time the Sauer family sold the property in the 1930s, they had lived there for five generations and suffered numerous tragedies: one suicide, one infant death, one child drowned in the swimming pool, and another killed in a train accident.

None of the ensuing owners stayed in the old Sauer place for very long, each one reporting a series of intense and disturbing manifestations. Lights reportedly move through the house and across the lawn. Laughing, weeping, and shouting emanate from the walls. Strange noises echo from the attic. The fireplace grates shake and rattle. A woman's voice sings somewhere in the distance. A ghostly, female figure has been seen in the cupola. When psychics were called in to investigate during the 1980s, they confirmed the hauntings and captured glowing orbs on film. Because of the intense activity and also legal and code problems, Sauer Castle now sits empty and forlorn. Basic structural repairs were carried out in 2000, but the house's future remains uncertain. In the meantime, neighbors and passersby continue to report strange activity around the property.

Sauer Castle is closed to the public. Entry to the property is strictly forbidden as of this writing. The house is surrounded by a security fence with trespass warnings.

STRAWBERRY HILL MUSEUM
720 N. 4th Street
Kansas City, KS 66101
(913) 371-3264
www.strawberryhillmuseum.org

In 1887, attorney John Scroggs and his wife Margaret built a magnificent forty-two-room, Queen Anne–style mansion on a bluff overlooking the Kansas and Missouri rivers. They named their dream home Strawberry Hill. For the next two generations, the Scroggs family lived happily in their mansion, only selling it in 1919 when it overwhelmed their dwindling needs. The house was sold to the Sisters of St. Francis, who were seeking a site in which to open an orphanage. Renamed St. John's Children's Home, the mansion was enlarged and continued to serve the greater good until 1987, when it was opened as the Strawberry Hill Museum.

At least four entities are known to haunt this grand old house. One of them has been identified as James Cruise, husband to one of the Scroggs daughters, who lived in the house in the early twentieth century. Cruise only appears on the third floor, where he has been spotted numerous times, at least once hiding in the back of a storage closet, frantically waving his hands to ward off the living. On the second floor, an unknown female presence lives in the master bedroom. Music and singing have been heard here, probably remnants of the time when the nuns of St. Francis lived in the house. Alone on the first floor is the entity of a young girl who is seen rocking in a chair in the tower room. The most prevalent and ambulatory ghost is known as the "Lady in Red." Wearing a red dress of 1940s design and sporting a bright red shock of hair, this amazingly solid apparition has been spotted in numerous rooms and even outside the house, where she always asks the same question after greeting people with a friendly "hi there." The question is, "Where is the house of the priest?" Investigations of old records and reported psychic contact with the ghost indicates that she came to St. John's looking for help after a botched abortion attempt left her bleeding to death. It appears that the poor woman is still looking for the priest in the hope of absolution, seven decades after her untimely death. The staff of Strawberry Hill is more than happy to discuss their ghostly residents.

Strawberry Hill Museum is open Saturday and Sunday from 12:00 P.M. to 5:00 P.M. Midweek tours are available on advance request. The house is closed from the last week in October through the Saturday before Thanksgiving. Entry fees apply.

MICHIGAN

FELT ESTATE
6597 138th Avenue
Holland, MI 49423
Mail: c/o Laketown Township
4334 Beeline Road
Holland, MI 49423
(616) 335-3050
www.feltmansion.org

Dorr Felt only had one big idea, but in its day it was a real money-maker. Felt's invention, the comptometer, was an early hand-cranked version of a calculator. About the size of a portable typewriter, the comptometer became an indispensable tool for secretaries and bookkeepers everywhere. The more comptometers there were adding up figures, the more money was adding up in Felt's bank account. In 1925, he built a seventeen-thousand-square-foot Colonial Revival–style summer home for his family near Holland, Michigan, far from the congestion of his native

Chicago. Tragically, only six weeks after the house was completed in August 1928, Felt's wife Agnes died. Eighteen months later, Felt joined her.

In 1949, the Felt family sold the summer home, and over the ensuing years it was used as a seminary, a convent, and a state police headquarters. After it was placed in the National Register of Historic Places, local preservation groups marked it as a prime candidate for restoration. Something about the renovation work must have shaken up some unknown spirits in the old house, because in 2001, when work was still going on, some very curious things began to happen. In the third-floor ballroom, human shadows appeared out of nowhere and moved in groups of one and two across the walls before vanishing as suddenly as they appeared. In the room that had been Agnes's bedroom, the French doors leading to the sunroom slammed open of their own accord. On hot, still days, when the sunroom's windows were closed, a chilling blast of cold air was emitted. Now open for tours and special events, the Felt mansion still experiences these strange and inexplicable occurrences.

Felt Estate is open for tours from the last week of May through the first week of October, Monday through Wednesday from 1:00 P.M. to 5:00 P.M. Entry fees apply.

NATIONAL HOUSE INN BED AND BREAKFAST
102 Parkview Street
Marshall, MI 49068
(269) 781-7374
www.nationalhouseinn.com

The National House Inn has been many things over the course of its 180-year history. Originally built in 1835 by Col. Andrew Mann, the house served as his home, an overnight stop for stagecoaches traveling between Detroit and Chicago, and a local meeting place. By 1878, Mann was dead and the hotel business had declined, thanks largely to the swiftly growing railroad. The building was demoted from its former dignified status to a factory for manufacturing windmills and farm wagons. In 1902, it underwent its first major restoration when it was converted into luxury apartments, and during the 1920s, parts of the basement were used as a speakeasy.

By 1976, the building again needed a full restoration. At that time it was converted to its current use as a bed-and-breakfast inn. Only then did the old house's one and only ghost appear. Manifesting herself as a fully formed entity, the so-called Lady in Red has appeared before staff and guests as she roams silently through both floors of the house. Given the building's long and varied history, it is small wonder that no one knows who she is or from exactly what time period she comes. Nevertheless, she makes her presence known with a fair degree of regularity.

National House Inn Bed and Breakfast is open all year.

BOWERS HARBOR INN
13512 Peninsula Drive
Traverse City, MI 49684
(231) 223-4222
www.bowersharborinn.net

Genevieve Stickney had problems. Specifically, she had problems with her weight and emotional stability. When her husband, J. W., built their sprawling summer home on a hill near Traverse City, Michigan, in 1885, she was little more than plump, but over the years poor Genevieve put on so much weight that she was unable to go up and down stairs by herself. To accommodate her needs, J. W. installed an elevator. Eventually, however, Genevieve's weight ballooned to the point where they had to hire a full-time nurse to look after her. Genevieve was understandably frightened that J. W. would abandon her for someone slimmer, but it wasn't until after her husband's death that she learned the someone was her nurse. J. W. left all of his money to the other woman. In despair, Genevieve hanged herself in the elevator shaft.

The lovely house passed through a series of owners until 1959, when it became the Bowers Harbor Inn. Along with the house, the restaurateurs inherited the ghostly entities of both Genevieve and

J. W. Stickney. J. W. usually appears as nothing more than a misty form, but has been known to materialize and is seen smiling in the old elevator. An occasionally levitating plate of food from one of the tables is credited to the invisible J. W. He always puts it back down without spilling anything. Genevieve, on the other hand, is just a bit vicious and is blamed for throwing kitchen utensils through the air and slamming doors shut with a crashing thud. Sometimes she appears in what was once her personal mirror, now located on the second floor; she particularly enjoys peeking over the shoulder of the person looking at their reflection and vanishing when they turn around. No one is quite sure which of the Stickneys makes the old elevator raise and lower by itself, even when the power is shut off, or who makes the knocking sounds that emanate from the walls and closets.

Bowers Harbor Inn is a full-service restaurant open all year for dinner only. The hours are Sunday through Thursday from 5:00 P.M. to 10:00 P.M. and Friday and Saturday from 5:00 P.M. to 11:00 P.M.

MINNESOTA

GLENSHEEN, THE HISTORIC CONGDON ESTATE
3300 London Road
Duluth, MN 55804
(218) 726-8910 or (888) 454-4536
www.glensheen.org

Chester Congdon had piles of money. In fact, at the time of his death in 1916, he was the richest man in Minnesota. Having accrued this fortune in a variety of enterprises, including iron mining, banking, land speculation, and a lucrative law practice, he used some of his earnings to build a house. Congdon began construction of the thirty-nine-room mansion known as Glensheen in 1905. Three years later the house was finished. Eight years after that, Chester died. The palatial estate, along with a hefty $40 million, passed to his youngest daughter, Elizabeth.

Elizabeth never married, but in 1932, she adopted a girl who became known as Marjorie Congdon. Marjorie, as it turned out, was violently crazy. In 1977, the eighty-three-year-old Elizabeth and her night nurse, Velma Pietila, were brutally murdered; Elizabeth was smothered with a pillow in her bedroom and Velma was bludgeoned to death with a candlestick on the second-floor landing. Marjorie's second husband, Roger Caldwell, was tried and convicted for the murders. In a separate trial, Marjorie was acquitted of aiding and abetting.

The house, in accordance with Elizabeth's will, was turned over to the University of Minnesota. Despite the notoriety of the murders and a $40,000 a year heating bill, the house was opened as a museum in 1979, but by then it was already haunted by the spirits of poor, murdered Elizabeth and Velma. Employees and visitors have spotted the two women roaming the halls, and their shadowy figures have been seen in the basement. Others have observed them peering out of the upstairs windows. On the spots where the two women were murdered, people experience feelings of dread and panic. As of this writing, Marjorie Congdon is in prison for arson and computer fraud.

Glensheen is open from the last week in May until mid-October, seven days a week, from 9:00 A.M. to 5:30 P.M. From mid-October until the third week of May, it is open Saturday and Sunday only from 9:30 A.M. to 3:30 P.M. Glensheen offers several tours; the last tour of the day begins ninety minutes before closing. Group tours of ten or more should be booked ahead. Entry fees apply.

LEDUC HISTORIC ESTATE
1629 Vermillion Street
Hastings, MN 55033
(651) 437-7055
www.dakotahistory.org/LeDuc/home.asp

The LeDuc mansion is a truly stunning example of the Gothic Revival style of architecture. Its construction cost was estimated at $5,000 in 1862 but soared to $30,000 before it was completed. Like so much in Gen. William LeDuc's life, his house outstripped his means. LeDuc worked hard for himself, his wife, and their four children, yet never quite managed to get ahead in spite of high-profile jobs, such as the first U.S. secretary of agriculture in the late 1870s. When his wife Mary died in 1904 at the age of seventy-five, LeDuc and his youngest daughter, Alice, turned to the popular practice of spiritualism, which involved attempts to contact the deceased through a medium.

By 1930, most of the LeDuc family had passed away and the fine house was sold to Carroll Simmons, an antiques dealer who lived there until 1958, when he in turn sold it to the Minneapolis Historical Society. Simmons believed the house was haunted, and he was up front about the activity probably being the work of William and Alice LeDuc. It took the historical society more than a quarter century to restore the house. By the time it opened as a museum in 2005, many people felt that Simmons's spirit had joined the general and his daughter in the old house. Doors throughout the house open and close by themselves, cold spots are evident here and there, and objects are reportedly moved from place to place without human intervention.

LeDuc Historic Estate is open from the last weekend in May through November 1, Wednesday through Saturday from 10:00 A.M. to 5:00 P.M. and Sunday from 1:00 P.M. to 5:00 P.M. Tours begin every ninety minutes from opening. Entry fees apply.

FOREPAUGH'S RESTAURANT

276 S. Exchange Street
St. Paul, MN 55102
(651) 224-5606
www.forepaughs.com

Joseph Forepaugh had a good life. In the 1860s, he owned the largest dry goods business in St. Paul, dealing in fabric, clothing, and household items. He also had a wife and two daughters who loved him and a fine, big house with well-manicured lawns and gardens. He also had a roving eye, and around 1885, he began an affair with his housemaid Molly. Forepaugh's wife, Mary, caught the pair in bed. In a fury, she dismissed the maid and laid down the law to her husband. Terrified that she would be unable to find a new employer, Molly hanged herself on the third floor from a chandelier in a bay window off the ballroom. Joe, with his life and reputation now under a very dark cloud, sold his house and took Mary and the family to Europe for three years. By the time they returned, he was even more depressed. Despite his flourishing business, Forepaugh insisted he was going broke, and in July 1892, at the age of fifty-eight, he calmly walked to the local park and shot himself.

Numerous families lived in the Forepaugh mansion over the ensuing years. In 1983, it was converted into an upscale French restaurant and named for its original owner. The name is particularly apt, because Joseph Forepaugh never really left the place. Neither did Molly the maid. On several occasions, the figure of Joe has been seen in the restaurant area and there is little doubt it is him; he looks just like his portrait that still hangs in the house. Molly has been seen and heard on the third floor and makes occasional appearances at wedding receptions held in the restaurant. In 1989, her arm was even photographed materializing from the staircase. There is also the sound of a woman singing lullabies on the third floor and the sound of feet walking through the old ballroom when no one is there. On one occasion, when the staff thought the noise was caused by an intruder, the police came with a K-9 dog that refused to go up the stairs.

Forepaugh's Restaurant is open for lunch Monday through Friday from 11:30 A.M. to 2:00 P.M., for dinner Monday through Saturday from 5:30 P.M. to 9:30 P.M., on Sunday for brunch from 10:30 A.M. to 1:30 P.M., and on Sunday for dinner from 5:00 P.M. to 8:30 P.M.

GIBBS MUSEUM OF PIONEER AND DAKOTAH LIFE
2097 W. Larpenteur Avenue
St. Paul, MN 55113
(651) 646-8629
www.rchs.com/gbbsfm2.htm

Jane and Herman Gibbs were just ordinary people. She had been raised on the Minnesota prairie near what is now Minneapolis and he had been a schoolteacher in Indiana. They met in Illinois in 1847, and despite the fact that Herman was fourteen years older than Jane, the pair fell in love and were married. Together they moved back to Minnesota, where they bought a 160-acre farm and built a log-and-sod cabin in which to start their life together. The land was fertile and they soon had a thriving business growing vegetables and selling them in the marketplace in St. Paul. By 1867, they had vastly expanded and improved the cabin to accommodate their five children, but their life was saddened that year when their nine-year-old son, William, died of smoke inhalation while helping his father fight a grass fire. Still, the family persevered. Herman died in 1891, Jane in 1910, and the farm passed to their fifty-five-year-old daughter Abbie.

In 1943, the farm was sold to the University of Minnesota, and six years later, it was taken over by the local historical society, which opened it to the public. We are unsure how long the spirit of little William Gibbs has been haunting the only home he ever knew, but his small footsteps are often heard in the hallway behind the kitchen. Sometimes he rocks in the family rocking chair and other times he has been seen peering out of one of the windows. He likes to open and close doors, particularly in his mother's kitchen, and sometimes, late at night, he opens the locked cabinets where his old toys are stored, spreads them out on the floor, and plays with them. Like many children, he never learned to put his toys away when he finishes with them.

Gibbs Museum of Pioneer and Dakotah Life is open from May 1 through October 31, Tuesday through Sunday from 12:00 P.M. to 4:00 P.M. and weekday mornings by appointment. Entry fees apply.

MISSOURI

HARRY S. TRUMAN NATIONAL HISTORIC SITE
223 N. Main Street
Independence, MO 64050
(818) 254-9929 or (818) 254-7199
www.nps.gov/HSTR

President Harry S. Truman was feisty and outspoken, but he continues to be well thought of by people of most political persuasions. It's hard to think of a former president as anything other than a professional politician, yet when Truman married Bess Wallace in 1919, he didn't even have enough money to rent a decent apartment, let alone buy a house. Consequently, they moved in with Bess's widowed mother, the notoriously difficult Margaret Wallace. Somehow, between trying to start a business and then becoming a fledgling politician, Truman never made enough money to buy a house of his own. During his years in Washington, he would return to his mother-in-law's house in Independence when he could.

At about the same time his tenure as president ended in 1953, Margaret Wallace passed away and Harry and Bess retired to the only other home they had known for thirty-five years. Even once he was out of politics, Truman was a popular public figure. News cameras followed him on his daily walks, cane in hand, sporting his Stetson hat as he smiled and waved and discussed politics with a reserved and folksy wisdom. Truman died in 1972 and his beloved Bess followed him ten years later.

The house became a national historic site, and thanks to the family's frugality, nothing much changed in more than a half century, except the kitchen, which had been updated in the 1950s. Maybe it is because the house has remained so very much like the Trumans left it that the president has been drawn back. Or maybe Harry Truman is simply no more willing to be told what to do, or where to go, in death than he was in life. In either case, the recognizably clear form of Truman has been seen sitting in his favorite chair by both staff and visitors alike. The smell of his favorite brandy has been detected fairly frequently, and some people even claim to see him striding down the sidewalk, dressed as usual and grinning broadly. Harry Truman was, and evidently still is, just that kind of guy.

Harry S. Truman National Historic Site is open seven days a week from 8:30 A.M. to 5:00 P.M. It is closed Thanksgiving, Christmas, and New Year's Day. Entry fees apply.

JAMES FARM
21216 James Farm Road
Kearney, MO 64060
(816) 736-8500
www.jessejames.org

The little one-story farmhouse looks peaceful enough today, but through much of the nineteenth century it saw more than its share of violence. Robert and Zerelda James were friendly people. They were full-time farmers, and he was a part-time preacher. When Robert died, Zerelda remarried. When her second husband died, she remarried again. In total she bore eight children, two of whom are well known today, sons Frank and Jesse.

Things might have turned out differently for the James boys had Union troops not raided the farm during the Civil War. After burning several nearby farms, soldiers lynched Jesse's stepfather and whipped Jesse mercilessly when he tried to intervene. In retaliation, Jesse joined a group of Confederate raiders commanded by the notorious William Quantrill. Later, after the war, he and Frank turned to crime. Years later, after Jesse and Frank's outlaw careers were well underway, Pinkerton detectives raided the farm, tossing dynamite through the windows. Jesse and Frank weren't there, but their brother Archie was killed and Zerelda lost a hand. In 1882, Jesse was murdered by his friend and fellow gang member, Bob Ford, and his body was returned to the family farm where Zerelda guarded her son's grave for the rest of her life.

In 1978, the old James farm became a museum. Once it opened, word of the hauntings began to spread. Cold spots are still felt in the house, strange flickering lights move past the windows after the place has been closed for the night, and staff and visitors often report feeling intensely ill at ease. Phantom faces have been photographed peering out through the windows and the sounds of phantom horses, stomping their hooves and snuffling, have been heard at the edge of the nearby woods early in the morning.

James Farm is open seven days a week, May through September, from 9:00 A.M. to 4:00 P.M. October through April, Sunday hours are reduced to 12:00 P.M. to 4:00 P.M., but other days remain the same. The site is closed on major holidays. Admission fees apply.

LA MAISON GUIBOURD-VALLÉ
4th and Merchant Streets
St. Genevieve, MO 63670
(573) 883-7544
www.stegenevievemissouri.com/guibourdvallehouse.htm

No one knows who built this simple, one-and-a-half-story frame house in 1784 when St. Genevieve was still Spanish territory. Its first recorded owners were the family of a French merchant named Jacques Dubreuil Guibourd, who purchased the house in 1806. The family continued to live there for the next one hundred years. The house changed hands in 1906 and again in 1931, when it was bought by the Vallé family, but up until then there was no indication that anything unusual was going on in the old structure.

The hauntings apparently started in 1939, when Jules Vallé was confined to bed after eye surgery. Although his vision had recovered, Vallé had to remain immobile and in semidarkness until he had completely healed. One day, Jules inexplicably caught the sweet scent of honeysuckle, and when he turned his head slightly, he saw the figures of three men dressed in Spanish military uniforms of the late eighteenth century standing next to his bed. At least they seemed to be standing; it was hard to tell because they only existed from the waist up. Jules's wife, Anne-Marie, didn't seem in the least shocked; she and the maid had been hearing phantom footsteps in the servants quarters for years.

In 1949, Jules Vallé passed away and only two months later Anne-Marie was awakened by the sound of someone apparently destroying the bedroom where her late husband had convalesced. Not surprisingly, no one was there and nothing was amiss in the room. In 1972, following Anne-Marie's death, the house became a museum and since then the strange occurrences have continued unabated, although they only take place occasionally. The long-dead Spaniards have reappeared, as have the mysterious footsteps. A ghostly presence plays the same song over and over on the old harpsichord, and a man's voice has been heard to shout "Hey!" Dogs are terrified of entering the house.

La Maison Guibourd-Vallé is open daily April through October from 10:00 A.M. to 5:00 P.M. and November through December from 12:00 P.M. to 4:00 P.M. January through March it is open only for special events and prearranged group tours. It is closed on major holidays. Entry fees apply.

LEMP MANSION
3322 DeMenil Place
St. Louis, MO 63118
(314) 664-8024
www.lempmansion.com

In 1980, *Life* magazine declared the Lemp Mansion to be one of the most haunted houses in America. For anyone already familiar with the place, this hardly came as a revelation. Built in 1868, this thirty-three-room mansion served as home to the Lemp family for three generations. First in occupancy was William Lemp, inheritor of his father's thriving brewing business. Suffering from clinical depression, Lemp lost interest in his business, and in 1904, he shot himself in the parlor. His son, William Jr., inherited the house and business, but in 1920, his sister Elsa shot herself in her second-floor bedroom. Two years later, with the onset of prohibition, William Jr. was forced to sell the brewery, and like his father before him, he shot himself in the parlor. The mansion then passed to his brother Charles, who not only inherited the house but also William's son with Down syndrome. Terrified of the scandal associated with having a mentally deficient child, the family kept the boy sequestered on the third floor for his entire life; he died there in 1947. A year later, Charles shot his dog in the basement, then died himself in 1949.

The Lemp family thus came to an end and their mansion became a boardinghouse that slowly slipped into a disreputable state, partially because of the inexplicable ghostly activity. In 1975, the house was rescued and turned into a bed-and-breakfast inn with a restaurant. Still, the hauntings continued unabated. Throughout the house the sound of feet can be heard, and on the second floor, guests hear the sound of someone kicking in a door. On the main stairway, floating orbs have been seen and photographed, and in the back stairway, a dog can be heard panting and dragging its chain. On the third floor, a childlike voice invites visitors to "come play with me." Toys left there are always moved. On the first floor, the piano plays ragtime music by itself. Drinks and empty glasses move around of their own accord. In the basement dining room, where more orbs have been seen, tables and settings move by themselves. In the women's bathroom, the lifelike apparition of a man's face peers over the walls of the stalls. Investigated numerous times, there seem to be five or six entities haunting the Lemp Mansion.

Lemp Mansion offers overnight rooms and a full-service restaurant, which is open to the public. They regularly host murder mystery dinner theater and special Halloween events.

NEBRASKA

BROWNVILLE HISTORICAL SOCIETY
412 Main Street
P. O. Box 1
Brownville, NE 68321
(402) 825-6001
www.brownville-ne.com

When former Civil War captain B. H. S. Bailey moved his family to Brownville in 1876, he found a thriving community with aspirations of becoming the new state capital. Although Brownville had been founded in 1854, it already had a population of thirteen hundred by the time it hosted the Nebraska State Fair in 1870 and 1871. It was both the county seat and an important port on the Missouri River. Encouraged by Brownville's progress, Bailey built a fine Gothic Revival–style mansion with seven heavily decorated gables to adorn its roofline. It was exactly the sort of home the town needed to keep up its image as a pacesetter in largely rural Nebraska. Unfortunately Brownsville's future was not all Bailey and his neighbors had hoped. By 1885, the railroad had bypassed the town and the county seat had been moved elsewhere. In the years after his death, Bailey's house, along with much of Brownville, deteriorated.

In 1959, the local historical society purchased Bailey's house, restored it, and opened it to the public as a museum. What they may not have known was that at least one unidentified former occupant, who had obviously been a music lover, still resided there. In the parlor stands a piano at which a shadowy figure has been seen intently bent over the keys, silently hammering out some long-forgotten tune. On other occasions, even when the ghost is not present, the strains of nineteenth-century piano music can be heard drifting through the house. Brownville may now only have a population of 150 people, but with thirty-two houses in the National Register of Historic Places, and at least one musically inclined ghost in residence, it still attracts a sizeable number of tourists.

Brownville Historical Society is open in May and September on Saturday and Sunday only from 1:00 P.M. to 5:00 P.M. From June 1 through August 31, it is open seven days a week from 1:00 P.M. to 5:00 P.M. Admission fees apply.

FORT SIDNEY MUSEUM
AND POST COMMANDER'S HOME
1153 6th Avenue
Sidney, NE 69162
(308) 254-2150

The town of Sidney was established in 1867 by the Union Pacific Railroad when they needed to have a way station between their depots in North Platte, Nebraska, and Cheyenne, Wyoming. Because of the importance of the railroad, the U.S. government immediately built Fort Sidney next to the railroad encampment with the intent of protecting the workers and miles of rail from marauding Indians.

The true importance of the fort, however, came with the discovery of gold. During the 1870s, Sidney was a boomtown boasting eighty-nine saloons. Among its frequent visitors were Wild Bill Hickock, Sam Bass, Whispering Smith, and Butch Cassidy. Between the daily shipments of gold and the hundreds of miners, gamblers, and disreputable characters, it was all the Army could do to maintain order. It would be logical to assume that the haunting of the Post Commander's House had some connection to the lawlessness in the town, but the truth is far more mundane. In 1885, only one year after a new commanding officer's house was built, the young wife of one of the officers was carrying an armload of laundry up the steep back stairs of the house. Unable to see her feet, she tripped, fell backward down the stairs, and broke her neck. When her grief-stricken husband found her body, he immediately ordered the stairway boarded up.

The hauntings began later, in the 1930s, when visitors first reported hearing the sound of someone walking up a set of stairs, followed by a heavy falling sound. There were no stairs to be seen, of course, so the matter was doubly mysterious. It was not until 1975 that workmen discovered the hidden stairs behind a pantry. The stairway has now been restored, but access is blocked by a wooden gate. No one has used the old stairs in more than 120 years, with the exception of the occasional workman *and* the spirit of the unfortunate woman who can still be heard endlessly climbing the steep stairs, tripping, and tumbling to her death.

Fort Sidney Museum and Post Commander's Home is open from Memorial Day through Labor Day from 9:00 A.M. to 11:00 A.M. and 1:00 P.M. TO 3:00 P.M. There is also a special Christmas open house. Admission is free.

OGALLALA MANSION ON THE HILL
Keith County Historical Society
N. Spruce Street and 10th Street
P. O. Box 5
Ogallala, NE 69153
(308) 289-2954
www.ogallalamansiononthehill.com

Almost from the day it was completed in 1887, Ogallala's Brandhoffer home was referred to locally as the "Mansion on the Hill." There is no question how it got its moniker: With ten spacious rooms heavily decorated with ornate plaster moldings, fireplaces trimmed in cherrywood, and hand-decorated tiles, it was the finest house Oglalla would ever see. At the time, it probably seemed like a fairly pretentious house for a widower with only one child and whose job was that of a humble cashier in the local bank. But Lawrence Brandhoffer had been around. A native of Pennsylvania, he had lived and worked in Iowa and three other towns in Nebraska before moving to Ogallala, and he had obviously saved up some money along the way. Curiously, only one year after building his mansion, Brandhoffer sold the house to his boss at the Keith County Bank. Over the years, the Mansion on the Hill would serve as the home for four different families, including a local mayor, before being converted to a World War I–era hospital and then apartments.

By the time the Brandhoffer mansion became the home of the local historical society, it had also picked up some very odd phenomena, some of which are attributed to its proximity to Ogallala's old "Boot Hill" cemetery, just a few blocks away. Late at night, when visitors and staff have all gone home and the house is dark, ghostly lights can be seen moving around the back rooms. Even during the day, employees and guests occasionally spot an unexplained, shadowy figure moving through the house's hallways. Photos taken from the exterior of the house show glowing orbs flitting around inside the second-floor windows.

Ogallala Mansion on the Hill is open from Memorial Day through mid-September. Tuesday through Saturday hours are 9:00 A.M. to 12:00 P.M. and 1:00 P.M. to 4:00 P.M. Sunday hours are 1:00 P.M. to 4:00 P.M. It is closed on Mondays. Offseason tours can be arranged by advance notification. Admission fees apply.

NORTH DAKOTA

SAGE HILL BED AND BREAKFAST/COUNTRY INN
2091 33rd Street NE
Anamoose, ND 58701
(701) 465-0225
http://sagehillnd.com

Well into the early twentieth century, the vast majority of North Dakota was still uninhabited, so it was a major accomplishment in 1928 when local businessman Col. Samuel White convinced the citizens of two tiny communities, Martin and Anamoose, to build a progressive school. In addition to two classrooms and living quarters for the two teachers, the redbrick school boasted a hot lunch program, wind-generated electrical power, six horse-drawn school buses, and showers for the students at a time when most North Dakota homes lacked running water. Heat was provided by a wood-fired boiler, and it was this that caused tragedy when it exploded, claiming the life of one male student and the district school superintendent. The damage was repaired and the school continued in use until 1968, but after its closure it was generally allowed to fall into disrepair.

In 1996, the schoolhouse was converted for use as a bed-and-breakfast inn. During renovations, the specter of the long-dead superintendent first made itself known and ghostly activity has continued ever since. The smell of the superintendent's cigar is occasionally detected, unexplained shadows move through the basement, cold spots occur at several locations, and small objects disappear and reappear in places where they should never have been. The sound of moaning has also been heard in the basement.

Sage Hill Bed and Breakfast/Country Inn is open all year. The restaurant is open to the general public for lunch and dinner with twenty-four-hour advance notification.

OHIO

FRANKLIN CASTLE CLUB
4308 Franklin Boulevard
Cleveland, OH 44113
www.franklincastleclub.com

Logic dictates that there is no such thing as an evil house; people can be evil, but buildings are neutral. Then there is the Tiedemann house. Long known as Franklin Castle, this thirty-room, four-story Gothic Revival mansion, complete with secret passages, hidden rooms, and gargoyle-topped turrets, was the creation of Hannes Tiedemann, a German immigrant who made a small fortune in banking. In 1865, when Tiedemann built the house, everything seemed fine, but fifteen years later, it was obvious that something was terribly wrong. In a matter of three years, the family had buried four children and one adult. Then one youthful relative, a thirteen-year-old niece, simply disappeared from the house. By 1909, the entire family had died, and their former home now attracted a series of unsavory owners. In the 1920s, it was used as an illegal distillery and speakeasy. The next owners were a group of German socialists, who may actually have been Nazi spies; during their tenure, rumors of a twenty-victim mass murder began to circulate.

More recently, there have been many owners, but none have stayed long. The Romanos bought it in 1968, and the very day they moved in, their six children were playing with a ghost child on the third floor. When the Romanos called in a group of ghost hunters, one member fled in terror. By 1975, Sam Muscatello owned the house, and in a secret room at the end of a hidden passage, he found a gruesome cache of children's bones. Since then, the number and variety of paranormal events has been nothing short of mind-boggling. Chandeliers reportedly move in a circular motion. The sounds of footsteps, voices, and crashing glass are often heard. The phantom of a woman in a black dress wafts through the halls, stares from a tiny window in the tower, and shows up in photos and on film. The child spirit still lives on the third floor, glowing orbs appear in photos, and moving shadows creep along well-lit hallways.

Franklin Castle is a private club and is closed to the public. If you are interested in joining the club, visit their Web site. Two Cleveland ghost tour companies include the site on their rounds. Psychic Sonya's Haunted Tours can be contacted at (440) 775-1217. Haunted Cleveland Ghost Tours can be reached at (216) 251-0406; visit their Web site at www.hauntedcleveland.net.

KELTON HOUSE MUSEUM AND GARDEN
586 E. Town Street
Columbus, OH 43215
(614) 464-2022
www.keltonhouse.com

Many of the stories in this book involve violent death or some other trauma that leaves the deceased with unfinished business among the living. This is not the case with the Kelton House. If anything, the story of this house is unusual because of its normality. Fernando and Sophia Kelton built a fine townhouse in 1854, and there they had six children, five of whom lived to adulthood.

The family had a strong sense of morality and harbored fugitive slaves prior to and during the Civil War. Although the Keltons did not believe in war, their eldest son, eighteen-year-old Oscar, joined the Union and died fighting in Mississippi in June 1864. When peace was restored, Fernando went south to bring his son's body home. While taking the boy's coffin to the railroad station the wagon turned over, spilling Oscar's body into the road and leaving Fernando with a severe concussion. Ill and in shock, Fernando never recovered and only eighteen months later in 1866, he suffered a dizzy spell, fell from his third-floor office window, and died. In 1888, his widow died, and the house passed first to their son Edwin and then to his daughter Grace Bird Kelton. Grace never married, but she took the bold leap into the world of business, becoming a nationally recognized interior designer. One of Grace's favorite projects was restoring the family home to its 1860s appearance, and when she died in 1975, the house, along with four Kelton ghosts, became part of a museum.

The diminutive, semitransparent form of Sophia is most often seen in her bedroom, but she also appears throughout the house, sometimes waving at the staff from her bedroom window as they leave for the night. Husband Fernando is there, too, and although he prefers to remain invisible, he is evident to the touch when he accidentally bumps into a living guest. When Fernando does appear, he seems almost embarrassed and immediately vanishes.

Eighteen-year-old Oscar is usually seen outside, still dressed in his Union blues. The last of the Keltons, Grace, still tends to the decoration. When staff members move the furniture to the wrong location, Grace moves it back. Sometimes she rifles through the office files, getting them mixed up; if things aren't clean enough, she thoughtfully lays out the cleaning supplies. Both Grace and Sophia often materialize at social functions held in the house.

Kelton House Museum and Garden is open for tours every Sunday from 1:00 P.M. to 4:00 P.M. Tours can be arranged at other times by advance scheduling. Entry fees apply.

BUXTON INN

313 E. Broadway Street
Granville, OH 43023
(740) 587-0001
www.buxtoninn.com

People like a sense of home and familiarity, so maybe that's why, when a group of folks from Granville, Massachusetts, immigrated to the Ohio frontier in 1805, they named their settlement Granville. They built New England-style homes, and in 1812, when Orrin Granger came west from the old Granville to the new Granville, he built a combination home-tavern-inn and simply named it The Tavern. The Tavern changed hands, and names, many times over the next two centuries, but it has always remained in business. Everyone associated with it, both owners and customers, seems to love the place. They love it so much that many of them have chosen to stay there even after death.

The first ghost reported was original owner Orrin Granger. He appeared in the 1920s in the kitchen, where he stopped eating the last piece of pie long enough to chat with the son of the owner. Then there is the ghost of Maj. Horton Buxton, who owned the place from 1865 until 1905 and gave the building its current name. The blue-clad spirit of Ethel "Bonnie" Bounell, who owned the place from 1934 until her death in 1960, has also made appearances. In addition to these former owners, there are reports of former stagecoach drivers clustered around the fireplace in the basement, where they once spent the night, as well as unidentified, shadowy figures in Room 7 and in the basement. A ghost cat has been spotted; some people feel it jumping on their beds. An unidentified female in mid-nineteenth-century clothing is frequently seen, as is a young boy who sits near the stone wall of the tavern area. Finally, there is a ghost with a long beard and broad-brimmed hat, typical of the 1860s and 1870s, who has been seen on the staircase. None of this vast array of spirits has ever caused any trouble; they just seem to enjoy being here. The Buxton Inn has been ghost-hunted on several occasions, and the current owners and staff have no problem discussing their ghostly clientele. The total number of ghostly inhabitants ranges between twelve and fourteen.

Buxton Inn is a bed-and-breakfast inn and is open all year. The restaurant is open to the public for lunch Tuesday through Saturday 11:30 A.M. to 2:00 P.M. and for dinner Tuesday through Saturday 5:30 P.M. to 9:00 P.M. They are open for Sunday brunch 11:00 A.M. to 3:00 P.M. and Sunday dinner 4:00 P.M. to 9:00 P.M.

CHATEAU LAROCHE, THE HISTORIC LOVELAND CASTLE

12025 Shore Road
P.O. Box 135
Loveland, OH 45140
(513) 683-4686
www.lovelandcastle.com

Harry Andrews was a truly good man. He was one of those people most of us refer to as a romantic, the kind of person who knows we could be better than we are and dedicates his life to improving things for everyone. During World War I, Harry enlisted as a medic. When he saved the life of a British earl's son, he found himself the recipient of an honorary knighthood. This and his natural inclination toward romanticism and the looming ruins of medieval castles dotting England and Europe set the course of Harry's life, a course strengthened when he returned home to find that his girlfriend had dumped him for somebody else.

Publicly, Harry Andrews worked for a local newspaper and led a Boy Scout troop, but privately he was dedicated to the romantic ideals of medieval chivalry: truth, bravery, and honor. In 1927, he bought some land for use as a campground for the scouts, and two years later, he began building a stone structure for them to use as a shelter. Using bricks, stones from the local river, and handmade concrete blocks, Harry went to work. When he retired in 1955, he continued building, and by the time he passed away, he had completed a Norman-style castle, filled with medieval antiques. His former Scouts, and now their sons and grandsons, still keep Harry's castle, and his dream, alive.

Harry and two other entities still keep watch over his legacy. The dark shadow of Harry is seen moving up the grand staircase toward his old bedroom. A transparent female spirit, thought to be the late wife of a neighbor killed in an explosion in the late 1920s, has been spotted walking across the river, up the road to the garden, and then resting on the garage-top patio. A third spirit, believed to be that of a Viking attached to an ancient sword in Harry's weapons collection, dresses in a long cloak and helmet with a short sword strapped across his chest. It is possible that this is the oldest ghost in America. The massive chandelier in the great hall has been known to sway in time with music.

Chateau Laroche is open April through September, seven days a week from 10:00 A.M. to 4:00 P.M. It is open from October through March on Saturdays and Sundays only, from 10:00 A.M. to 4:00 P.M. In October, the site hosts a Haunted Halloween event. Entry fees apply.

SQUIRE'S CASTLE
River Road
North Chagrin Reservation
Cleveland Metroparks
Willoughby Hills, OH 44144
(216) 635-3200
www.clemetparks.com

Fergus Squire had everything a successful executive of the Standard Oil Company could want—everything except his own manor house. The British-born Squire had a fine home in Cleveland, a lovely if slightly neurotic wife, and good kids, yet he longed to have a country estate like those he remembered from his homeland. In 1890, he bought 525 acres of forest and meadow a few miles east of Cleveland and began work on the first phase of the planned estate, the gatehouse-lodge. Built to look like a tiny, three-story castle, it had all the amenities of home, including a trophy room for stuffed animal heads.

An avid hunter, Squire spent weekends and summer vacations at the estate and dragged his wife along, although she made it clear that she hated the house, country living, hunting, and being away from her friends and the city. Terrified by the nocturnal sounds of animals, she wandered around the house at night, carrying a small lantern and rechecking the locks on the doors and windows. Finally, after more than thirty years of nagging, Squire relented. In 1922, he sold the land and lodge to the Cleveland park system and gave up his dream of a country home. The park authorities, fearful of vandalism and injury, removed the interior and roof of the building, leaving only an empty shell.

It wasn't until the 1950s, after both Squire and his wife had died, that people began reporting a phantom figure walking past the second-floor windows carrying a lantern, despite the fact that there is no longer a second floor. Since then there have also been reports of a woman's screams coming from the building and shadowy apparitions wandering the grounds. Glowing orbs have been photographed outside the castle and in the nearby woods. The phantom is believed to be the late Mrs. Squire, still checking the window locks to keep out the ferocious rabbits and squirrels.

Squire's Castle and the surrounding park is open daily, all year, from dawn until dusk. Entry is free.

SOUTH DAKOTA

HISTORIC ADAMS HOUSE
22 Van Buren Avenue
Deadwood, SD 57732
(605) 578-3724
www.adamsmuseumandhouse.org

When W. E. Adams and his wife Alice bought the sandstone and shingle Queen Anne house in 1920, the building was already seventeen years old and Adams was sixty-six. The couple recently had lost one of their daughters through illness, and their surviving daughter had married and moved to California, so the ten-room house was probably more than they really needed; it was just too lovely to pass up. In 1925, Alice was diagnosed with cancer, and during a last trip to California to see her pregnant daughter, she passed away. The shock of her mother's death caused the girl to miscarry and then die herself. Suddenly, at the age of seventy-one, Adams was alone in the world. Amazingly, less than a year later, he married again—to a woman named Mary, who was only twenty-nine years old.

In 1936, Adams died at home of a stroke. Not wanting to remain alone in the big old house, Mary locked the doors and left, leaving everything exactly as it was. Mary insisted the hasty departure was purely practical and sentimental, but rumors abound that only days after Adams's death she began hearing him walking around on the second floor. Whatever the case, for the next fifty years, Mary made an annual pilgrimage back to Deadwood. She never spent the night there, however; she instead stayed at the Franklin Hotel. In 1987, the aging Mary sold her house for use as a bed-and-breakfast inn. The enterprise failed, but ten years later, the Adams house was purchased, complete with contents, by the city of Deadwood, which restored it and opened it as a museum in 2000. The sound of W. E. Adams's heavy boots can still be heard on the second floor, accompanied by the smell of his cigars. The rocking chair in second wife Mary's room sometimes rocks by itself; whether it is Mary or W. E. just taking a rest is unknown.

Hsitoric Adams House is open May through September daily from 9:00 A.M. to 5:00 P.M. and October through April on Tuesday through Saturday from 10:00 A.M. to 4:00 P.M. It is closed on winter holidays. Group tours require one month advance reservation. The house also hosts a variety of regular historical and cultural events, including an annual Halloween ghost tour of the property. Entry fees apply.

BULLOCK HOTEL

633 Main Street
Deadwood, SD 57732
(605) 578-1745 or (800) 336-1876
www.historicbullock.com/bull_hotel/index.php

The year 1876 was big for Deadwood. It celebrated the nation's centennial, the town's population quadrupled as a result of a gold strike the previous year, crime was rampant and rising, and James Butler "Wild Bill" Hickock was murdered while playing poker in Nuttall & Mann's Saloon. Only weeks prior to Wild Bill's murder, a former lawman named Seth Bullock rode into town with his partner, Sol Star. Sick of fighting and shooting, Bullock only intended to open a hardware store. When he arrived he was immediately offered the job of sheriff; he turned it down at first, but then changed his mind after Wild Bill's death.

While buddy Sol ran the hardware store, Bullock tamed Deadwood. At six feet in height and with a steely-eyed stare described as being "able to halt a rogue elephant," Seth was the man for the job. Over the years, Bullock and Star's business ventures prospered, too. In 1894, they decided the town needed an upscale hotel, a place where they both could live as well, so they built one. It immediately burned to the ground, but they just as quickly rebuilt and moved in. Seth Bullock loved his hotel so much that he and his family made Room 211 their home until he died in 1919.

The Bullock Hotel has always remained open, but by 1990, Deadwood was in danger of becoming a ghost town. With its population reduced to only eighteen hundred, Deadwood needed an infusion of life. Their solution was legalized gambling, and along with it came a major restoration of the Bullock Hotel. Whether inspired by the return to the 1894 look or the introduction of slot machines, which Bullock hated, he has been seen all over the hotel ever since. Photos taken in Room 211 show a white mist floating over Seth's bed. His fully formed entity has been seen all over the second and third floors. A lost little boy was once led to his room by a man "dressed like a cowboy," who he later identified as Bullock from a photo. Bullock is still unimpressed by idle employees; those not doing their jobs may wind up on the receiving end of flying glassware or dishes. One employee once saw an entire row of empty barstools move by themselves in the basement restaurant. Seth seems to have an unidentified companion; the ghost of a small girl about ten years old has been seen by numerous guests, and she is blamed for mischievously moving guests' clothing and turning faucets on and off.

Bullock Hotel is open all year. They have two restaurants and a bar that offer food and drink service for all meals, including Sunday brunch. There is also a casino on site.

A DAKOTA DREAM BED AND BREAKFAST
801 Almond Street
Hot Springs, SD 57747
(605) 745-4633 or (888) 881-4633
www.blackhillsguesthouse.com

Fred Evans was one of those men who grew up but never quite matured. Even as a rich businessman from Iowa, he still wanted a clubhouse for "the boys," so in 1891, he built one in Hot Springs. Fred spent his vacations there, and it was the venue of choice for him and his rowdy, debauched pals. Booze, gambling, and local ladies of the evening were always present. By 1916, a Spanish-style mansion called Villa Theresa had been built down the road by Chicago millionaire F. O. Butler. Whether Fred had grown too old to play or the new neighbors bought his clubhouse to get rid of him is unknown, but in 1925, Fred sold his guesthouse to the Butlers. The sprawling, five-thousand-square-foot guesthouse changed hands twice more between 1974 and 1990, when it was converted into a bed-and-breakfast, which it has remained ever since, now operating under the name A Dakota Dream.

The accounts of hauntings date back as far as about 1970 and include several figures who appear only on the staircase. First there is the very lifelike, but eerily pale, specter of a lovely woman in a late-nineteenth-century evening gown who takes a few steps before disappearing. There is also the image of a man who kneels on the stairs and peers threateningly through the spindles. The last, and most frightening, of the stairway ghosts is a transparent couple dressed in 1950s clothes (she wears a poodle skirt and bobby socks) who fight violently on the landing; their struggle ends when the man tosses her over the railing and they both dematerialize. There are also reports of blue orbs moving along the living room ceiling. Several people have reported awakening in the middle of the night to confront the disembodied face of F. O. Butler staring down at them from above the bed. None of these entities appears very often, but when they do their displays are evidently fairly spectacular.

A Dakota Dream Bed and Breakfast is open all year.

WISCONSIN

HEARTHSTONE HISTORIC HOUSE MUSEUM
625 W. Prospect Avenue
Appleton, WI 54911
(920) 730-8204
www.hearthstonemuseum.org

On the evening of September 30, 1882, Henry and Crimora Rogers turned on the lights in their new house. This doesn't exactly sound earth-shattering unless you know that theirs was the first house in history to be lighted by electrical power from a central generating station. Some months before, while Rogers was building his new house, he was also in talks with representatives from the Edison Light Company to purchase a generator for the company he managed, the Appleton Paper and Pulp Company, and a neighboring business, the Kimberly-Clark Paper Company. An Edison generator was installed in the Appleton Paper mill and power lines were run to both the Kimberly-Clark plant and the Rogers's new house on the hill above his firm. The family lived in their wonderful house for only eleven years before selling it. In 1900, it was sold again to an entrepreneurial philanthropist named A. J. Priest, who lived there until his death in 1930. The house was then converted into the Hearthstone Restaurant.

Priest may have been dead, but he seemed unable to leave his house, and his presence has been felt there ever since. The restaurant folded in 1986, and because of its aged condition, the building was slated for demolition. It was saved, however, by local preservationists, who restored the house, including the oldest electrical wiring system in America, and opened it as a museum. The restoration only heightened Priest's spectral presence. Staff and visitors to what is now known as the Hearthstone Historic House Museum often hear unexplained and inexplicable noises; some sound distinctly like a person sneezing. Nearly everyone who visits the house claims to experience the unsettling feeling of someone watching them, and the unseen observer does not always seem approving of the strangers who wander through his house.

Hearthstone Historic House Museum is open all year, Tuesday through Friday from 10:00 A.M. to 4:00 P.M. and Saturday from 11:00 A.M. to 4:00 P.M. Tours start every half hour. Groups of ten or more should phone ahead. The house is closed on major holidays. Admission fees apply.

GALLOWAY HOUSE AND VILLAGE
336 Old Pioneer Road
P.O. Box 1284
Fond du Lac, WI 54936
(920) 922-0991 or (920) 922-6390
www.fdl.com/history/galloway.iml

The Galloway family moved into the Fond du Lac area around 1854, farming the land and investing what little spare money they had in the vast stands of timber that covered much of the surrounding landscape. As their fortunes improved, they added to their small house, bit by bit, until 1880, when it had grown into a fine, thirty-room Italianate mansion with all of the Victorian decoration any middle-class family of that era could want. To add to their air of prosperity, the family even had their own display coffin, which was brought down from the attic when circumstances demanded a wake in the home, as was the custom of the day. After the wake, the coffin was put back upstairs and the deceased was buried in a more modest box. For three generations, the Galloways lived here; they moved away in 1926. Other families owned the property before it was purchased by the local historical society and turned into the centerpiece of an open-air museum, but it always has been referred to as the old Galloway place.

Somewhere along the way the house picked up a few residual residents. Visitors to the museum have reported hearing the sounds of children laughing and playing in the second-floor playroom, dishes rattling in the kitchen cupboards, and spectral voices chatting amiably among themselves. The director of the Fond du Lac Historical Society says she has never experienced any of these manifestations herself, but hopes they are real, adding, "We might get more tourists that way."

Galloway House and Village is open seven days a week from Memorial Day through Labor Day from 10:00 A.M. to 4:00 P.M. and weekends in September from 10:00 A.M. to 4:00 P.M. Entry fees apply.

HISTORIC 1856 OCTAGON HOUSE
276 Linden Street
Fond du Lac, WI 54935
(920) 922-1608
www.octagonhousefdl.com

Many of the properties in this book began as houses but have been converted to other uses over their years. The architectural oddity known as the Octagon House, on the other hand, began life in 1856 as a trading post on an Indian reservation. Simultaneous to its commercial use, the building served as a safehouse on the Underground Railroad; incorporated into its twelve-room structure were passages, a hidden room, and nine extensive underground tunnels, all of which can still be toured by visitors. Amazingly, although the building was converted into a private residence, even serving as the home of one of Fond du Lac's first mayors, all knowledge of the tunnels and passages had been lost until the house was rescued from demolition and restored in 1975.

From the Octagon House's earliest years as a private home, there were rumors that something was not quite right about it. Even today, doors open and close by themselves, unexplained shadows flit through the rooms, cold spots emerge, and footsteps can be heard on empty staircases. As is the case with many haunted houses, small items are often moved by unseen hands, but in the Octagon House, the spirits take their interference into the real world very seriously. On one occasion, the old spinning wheel, which was in an unoccupied room, was completely disassembled in a matter of minutes and its pieces scattered all over the floor. The only entity that manifests itself visually is the ghost of a young boy who has been seen in several different rooms. Late at night, ghostly lights move through the darkened house.

Historic 1856 Octagon House is open to the public April through October on Monday, Wednesday, and Friday from 1:00 P.M. to 5:00 P.M. A guided tour begins at 2:00 P.M. Groups of six or more can be accommodated or arrange for a Victorian dinner party. Special events are scheduled occasionally; check the Web site for details. Entry fees apply.

TALIESIN
5607 City Road C
Spring Green, WI 53588
(608) 588-7900 or (877) 588-7900
www.taliesinpreservation.org

Anyone familiar with the history of American architecture will immediately equate the name of this house with one of our country's most innovative architects, Frank Lloyd Wright. Architecture fans will be familiar with Wright's early Prairie-style houses and his masterpiece structures, Fallingwater near Pittsburgh and the Solomon R. Guggenheim Museum in New York City. Few remember the scandals that swirled around Wright, however, and made his own home, Taliesin, haunted. In 1903, Edwin Cheney hired Wright to design a home for him and his wife, Martha, known as Mamah. Wright and his wife, Catherine, became friends with the Cheneys, but by 1909, Frank and Mamah had gotten a little too close. They abandoned their spouses and children and ran off to Europe. On their return, Edwin Cheney divorced Mamah, allowing the children visitation rights. Catherine Wright, though, suspected that her notorious cheapskate husband would leave her penniless, so she refused to divorce him. Socially ostracized in 1911, Wright and Mamah fled Chicago and moved to Spring Green, where he built the house known as Taliesin.

In August 1914, Wright was away on a commission while Mamah's children were visiting her at the house. One evening, a workman who Wright had recently fired stormed into the house with an ax and murdered seven of the nine people present—Mamah, two of her children, and four workmen—before dousing the house with gasoline and setting it on fire. Firemen pulled the dead and dying from the wreckage and carried them to the guest-house, and it is here that the ghost of Mamah is still seen wandering through the rooms wearing a long white gown. Windows in the cottage open and close by themselves and lights mysteriously go on and off. In the main house, visitors report the scent of gasoline or smoke in the dining room. Children have reported seeing two spirit children wearing "funny clothes" in the house and playing on the lawn. Obviously, the long dresses and knee pants of the early twentieth century would look funny to a modern child. Children are no longer allowed inside Taliesin and the guides refuse to discuss the ghosts. The restored Taliesin is now a museum.

Taliesin is open May through October. The two-hour tours take place seven days a week at 12:00 P.M. and 3:00 P.M. Reservations are strongly recommended. Children under twelve are not permitted. Entry fees apply.

BRUMDER MANSION

3046 W. Wisconsin Avenue
Milwaukee, WI 53208
(414) 342-9767 or (866) 793-3676
www.brumdermansion.com

In the closing years of the Victorian era, George Brumder made a small fortune publishing German-language newspapers and books. Sharing the wealth with his loved ones, he built this grand eight-thousand-square-foot mansion in 1910 for his son George Jr. and daughter-in-law Henrietta and their eleven children. In the 1920s, the Brumders sold the house to a reputed Chicago mobster named Sam Picks, who used the impressive basement ballroom as a speakeasy. By the late 1930s, the property was sold again and became a respectable boardinghouse. Over the years, the big old house has been many things, but in 1997, it was completely restored and redecorated for use as a bed-and-breakfast inn. It was then that ghostly activity began.

At least three ghosts are known to inhabit the house and move freely through the rooms. The most haunted room is the Gold Suite, which is home to a relative of the Brumder family known as

Aunt Pussy, real name Susan, who was notorious for hating dogs. Guests who bring their dogs here experience nightmares telling them to get rid of the animals. A mirror in the bathroom was seen to lift itself off of its hook and float to the bathtub before crashing. Similarly, a framed, antique marriage certificate in the room became airborne before smashing. The deadbolt of the room has locked by itself as well. In the dining room, neatly laid silverware gets mysteriously scattered across the table. In George's Suite, an employee once watched as an electrical plug unplugged itself. In Marion's Room, towels levitate from the rail and an invisible hand bounces the mattress hard enough to awaken sleeping guests. The specter of a woman in early twentieth-century attire appears in the basement ballroom, now used as a theater, and a woman in a black dress has been seen floating down the main stairs, where the sound of a man's footsteps can also be heard around 4:00 P.M. on many days. Several EVPs have been taken in the house. It is worth noting that the current owners are avid paranormalists who enjoy sharing stories of their invisible lodgers with guests.

Brumder Mansion is a bed-and-breakfast inn that is open all year.

WEST

ALASKA

WASHINGTON

MONTANA

OREGON

IDAHO

WYOMING

NEVADA

UTAH

COLORADO

CALIFORNIA

ARIZONA

NEW MEXICO

HAWAII

ALASKA

JESSE LEE HOME
1824 Phoenix Road
P. O. Box 905
Seward, AK 99664
(907) 224-3080
www.jesseleehome.net

Establishing the identity of a particular entity, or entities, which haunt a building is always challenging, but in the case of the Jesse Lee Home it is literally impossible. From its construction in 1925 until its abandonment in 1964, this orphanage was the full-time residence of more than eight hundred children and nearly one hundred staff members. The original Jesse Lee School and Children's Home was established in 1890 in the tiny village of Unalaska, located far out in the Aleutian Islands. After the number of orphans quadrupled during the 1918 Spanish Flu pandemic, the facility was relocated to Seward for better access to supplies that came by ship from Seattle.

While some orphanages earned sinister reputations, the Jesse Lee seems to have been a model of loving care and superior education. Here, even without the attention of their own parents, the children felt loved, wanted, and safe—at least until Good Friday 1964. On that day a devastating earthquake struck the town of Seward. Several of the dormitories collapsed, killing more than a dozen children, and the main building was severely damaged. The orphanage was moved to Anchorage and the old facility was left to the mercy of time and weather. But ever since its abandonment, hundreds of visitors who have come to the old Jesse Lee Home have felt acutely aware that at least some of the children still inhabit the only home they ever knew.

The moment visitors approach the overgrown grounds they experience an almost overwhelming sense of sadness, but as they walk toward the main building this changes abruptly. From every direction comes the sound of children playing. The soft noise of a jump rope swishing against concrete is accompanied by laughing and giggling. Sometimes the sounds of a game of tag, indicated by dozens of running feet and little voices cheering, are heard. At other times, an invisible ball can be heard bouncing along the playground. None of the ghostly children have ever been seen, but their presence is undeniable.

Jesse Lee Home is currently undergoing restoration work, prior to being opened as a museum. It is not yet open to the public, but prospective visitors can call the local preservation office for information concerning occasional organized visits to the site.

ARIZONA

OLIVER HOUSE BED AND BREAKFAST
26 Sowles Avenue
Bisbee, AZ 85603
(520) 432-1900

In 1909, Edith Ann Oliver built this lovely large house as a residence for executives working for her husband's mining company. It was later transformed into a boardinghouse, and that's when the problems started. Over the years, at least twenty-seven people died in the house, many of them violently, and at least five of them are unable to leave.

The spirit of mining company employee Nathan Anderson occasionally appears outside Room 13, where he was shot through the head by an unknown assailant in February 1920. Then there is the sound of ghostly gunshots, often described as sounding like distant firecrackers, followed by running feet; this is possibly a remnant of the night when a local police officer shot his adulterous wife, her lover, and several guests in the parlor before fleeing the house only to turn the gun on himself. In the Purple Sage Room, shutters and doors open and slam shut of their own accord. In the Captain's Room, a disembodied voice has been heard to shout "get out!" The Plum Room has a moving cold spot and gives visitors the uneasy feeling of being watched. A far more benign and comforting spirit inhabits the Grandma Room, where the apparition of an old woman rests in a rocking chair, smiles sweetly, and winks at guests before she vanishes into thin air.

Investigated numerous times, the Oliver House also manifests cold spots and the sound of running water where pipes no longer exist. Numerous digital photos taken on the second floor have repeatedly produced cloudy, ghostlike anomalies. The Oliver House now operates as a charming bed-and-breakfast, so if you want to spend a night in a haunted house, with all the luxuries of home, your chances are about as good here as they are anywhere else.

Oliver House Bed and Breakfast is open all year. Bisbee has its own ghost tour; for further information call (520) 432-3308.

RIORDAN MANSION STATE HISTORIC PARK
409 W. Riordan Road
Flagstaff, AZ 86001
(928) 779-4395
www.azstateparks.com/Parks/RIMA/index.html

In 1898, the lumber-baron Riordan brothers, Timothy and Michael, built a magnificent forty-room, thirteen-thousand-square-foot duplex log mansion for themselves and their wives, Caroline and Elizabeth, who were also sisters. Although it was a log cabin, the house was painted in a popular Victorian color—pink. Life for the Riordan families was good, at least until Tim and Caroline's daughter, Anna, contracted polio. Caroline tended her daughter constantly, but despite her ministrations, Anna died.

Both daughter and mother still haunt the bedroom where Anna died. The Riordan house is now a museum and the centerpiece of the Riordan Mansion State Historic Park. Despite numerous reported sightings of Caroline and Anna in the second-floor bedroom, the staff consistently denies that the house is haunted.

Riordan Mansion State Historic Park is open November through April from 10:30 A.M. to 5:00 P.M. and May through October from 8:30 A.M. to 5:00 P.M. The park is closed on Christmas Day. There is an entry fee, which includes guided tours of both the house and grounds. Tours fill up quickly and advance reservations are strongly recommended.

CASEY MOORE'S OYSTER HOUSE
850 S. Ash Avenue
Tempe, AZ 85281
(712) 621-4291
www.caseymoores.com

Although it is now a popular restaurant and bar, Casey Moore's was built as a private home in 1910 by William Moeur, the brother of Arizona's second governor. Later the house degenerated into a brothel, and it was from this period that most of the ghosts seem to originate. True to their original profession, the fun-loving spirits like to flirt with customers and employees and tease the neighbors. They have been known to rearrange table settings, throw food and silverware on the floor, and laugh while they create general havoc.

One of the former prostitutes has been spotted at the foot of the stairs leading to the second floor and has been known to give those going upstairs a gentle shove from behind. Late at night, when the living customers have long departed, a long-dead couple has been seen dancing and laughing through the upstairs windows. Could it be William and Mary Mouer still enjoying their home, or is it one of the brothel girls entertaining a customer before getting down to business? During professional ghost hunts, disembodied voices have been recorded on tape and the image of a skull has inexplicably appeared on more than one photo taken inside the restaurant area.

Casey Moore's Oyster House is open all year.

BUFORD HOUSE BED AND BREAKFAST
113 E. Stafford Street
P. O. Box 98
Tombstone, AZ 85638
(520) 457-3969 or (800) 263-6762

Around 1882, a year or so after the Earp brothers and Doc Holliday shot it out with the Clanton gang near the O.K. Corral, local mine owner George Buford built a nice, two-story adobe house for himself and his dad near the center of Tombstone. Shortly thereafter, George started to court a young lady named Cleopatra. According to local legend, Cleopatra made the unforgivable mistake of allowing another man to walk her home one evening. Although it was apparently innocent, George was furious. When she came to George's house to apologize, he shot her twice before killing himself. Cleopatra recovered, but George's spirit, trapped by remorse, began haunting his old home.

Since then, the house has been owned by two sheriffs, a mayor, and the great John Wayne himself. All of them encountered George's ghost. The Buford House is now a bed-and-breakfast, where George continues to appear, both inside and outside. Knocking is heard in the walls, faucets and lights go on and off by themselves, and mysterious lights flit across the walls of the Wicker Room. Women seem to be particular favorites of George, and many female guests have felt an unseen hand stroke their hair or their necks. He sometimes even gives gentle swats to women on their bottoms. Occasionally, a lady's bedcovers are pulled from her sleeping body or she hears someone calling her by name. The Buford House is a great base for a tour of old Tombstone, so long as you don't mind sharing your room with the late, extraordinarily jealous George Buford.

Buford House Bed and Breakfast is open all year. While in Tombstone, don't miss the Old West Historic Ghost Tour on Friday, Saturday, or Sunday. Call (520) 266-9630 or visit www.oldwesthistoric ghosttours.com/default.html.

CALIFORNIA

JAMES STUART CAIN HOUSE
Bodie State Historic Park
P. O. Box 515
Bridgeport, CA 93517
(760) 647- 6445
www.bodie.com

Bodie, California, is one of America's best-preserved ghost towns. In the 1870s, its heyday, Bodie boasted thirty gold mines, seventy saloons, three breweries, a school, and ten thousand inhabitants. Now, all that remains are 168 abandoned buildings and homes, thousands of personal possessions, and about twelve souls—literally. Not one living person now inhabits Bodie.

The most famous of Bodie's haunted houses is the James Stuart Cain House, still inhabited by a Chinese maid who was so distraught at the shame of being fired that she committed suicide. Today she likes to appear in one of the upstairs bedrooms, where she smiles at children but takes a less friendly attitude toward grownups. Adults attempting to spend the night in the house say she climbs into bed with them, pressing down until they feel like they are smothering. Lights in the house go on and off by themselves and the sound of a long-gone music box can be heard playing. Other haunted houses in Bodie are the Gregory House, haunted by the ghost of an old woman in a rocking chair knitting an afghan, and the Mendocini House, where the smell of Mama Mendocini's cooking fills the kitchen while the sound of a children's party echoes from the next room. Other ghosts include a variety of former townsfolk and the apparition of a white mule.

Bodie State Historic Park is open between May and October from 8:00 A.M. to 7:00 P.M. There is no entry fee. Readers are advised not to visit Bodie during the winter, when snow can sometimes accumulate to twelve feet. Otherwise, be sure to get plenty of gas and food before going to Bodie, because there is nothing available there.

MADRONA MANOR WINE COUNTRY INN AND RESTAURANT

1001 Westside Road
Healdsburg, CA 95448
(707) 258-4003 or (800) 433-4231
www.madronamanor.com

The fine Victorian house now known as the Madrona Manor was built in 1881 by John Alexander Paxton, a wealthy businessman and early pioneer in the California wine industry. Even in its day, Madrona Knoll Rancho, as it was then known, was a showplace and it remained so until 1981, a century after its construction, when it was converted into a top-notch hotel, bar, and restaurant.

It was during renovations that workmen felt uncomfortable, as if they were being watched. By the time the Madrona Manor opened for business at least two ghosts were firmly ensconced in the building, both of them female and unidentified. One of them is a woman in her thirties, who wears a Victorian-era dress and haunts Room 101, where she sometimes appears next to the bed before moving to one of the chairs; there she takes a seat for a moment before vanishing. The other is an elderly woman, again in nineteenth-century garb, who is occasionally seen entering the dining room through the French doors; a few guests insist that she has spoken directly to them.

Madrona Manor Wine Country Inn and Restaurant is open all year.

STOKES RESTAURANT AND BAR

500 Hartnell Street
Monterey, CA 93940
(831) 373-1110
www.stokesrestaurant.com

This wonderful old adobe was built in 1833 as the one-room home of Benjamin Day. Four years later, British sailor James Stokes jumped ship carrying a box of medical supplies he had stolen from his vessel's cargo hold. With virtually no medical knowledge, he proceeded to pass himself off as a doctor and pharmacist. Because Monterey had no practicing physician, Stokes got more business than he could handle and among his many unfortunate patients was the local police commissioner, who died under Stokes's care. Oddly, Stokes promptly married the man's widow, Josefa Soto de Cano. In 1840, they bought and expanded the one-room mud-brick house, which now bears their name, to an impressive seven rooms.

Despite the frightening number of patients who died through his incompetence, including California governor Jose Figueroa, Stokes climbed the social ladder to become mayor of Monterey. Facts on Stokes's demise are sketchy, but local legend says his undoing came when two of his sons caught him molesting their sister. Rather than face frontier justice, Stokes took some of his own medicine and died in 1855. In the years that followed, the house changed hands frequently, until it was bought in 1890 by local movers and shakers Mortimer and Hattie Gragg. The Gragg house was the center of Monterey social life until Hattie's death in 1948, when it was converted into a restaurant; at this point, the stories of the hauntings began.

The restaurant may have changed hands a number of times since 1950, yet reports of apparitions have not abated since. In addition to the sounds of footsteps and a baby crying on the second floor, and the usual flickering lights and slamming doors, there are three distinct entities who have made appearances. One is Hattie Gragg, who is probably responsible for most of the occurrences upstairs. Downstairs, a man in mid-nineteenth-century clothes is assumed to be James Stokes. A woman who appears on the staircase is believed to be Josefa. In the main dining room, staff and customers report jerking at the chairs, cold spots, and a disembodied woman's voice calling them by their names and asking, "Excuse me, can you help me?"

Stokes Restaurant and Bar is open all year at 5:30 P.M. for dinner only.

WHALEY HOUSE MUSEUM
2476 San Diego Avenue
San Diego, CA 92110
(619) 297-7511
www.whaleyhouse.org

The ground at this fine house was probably haunted even before Thomas Whaley built it in 1856. Four years earlier "Yankee Jim" Robinson was hanged from a tree that once stood in what became the archway between the Whaleys' parlor and music room. The Whaley family could hear Jim's ghost stomping around the second floor and felt a choking sensation if they lingered in the archway too long. The Whaleys had their own tragedies to deal with, however. Their son, Tom Jr., died of scarlet fever at only seventeen months of age and his crying can still be heard in his bedroom, while the ghost of his spotted dog mopes around the doorway and runs in the yard. Years later, the daughter of one of the servants was accidentally choked to death by a clothesline; ever since then a little girl with red-blond hair has been seen in the kitchen and playing in the garden, where she sometimes pauses to smell the flowers. Eventually, Thomas Whaley and his wife joined their ghostly crew and are often spotted calmly going about their daily activities. Thomas wears his long black frock coat and his wife calmly rocks an unseen child in a rocking chair.

Since the Whaley house opened as a museum in 1960, the activity has only increased. There is the smell of bread baking in the kitchen, full-bodied apparitions, floating orbs of light, cold spots, the scent of both cigars and perfume, and the sounds of conversation, singing, whistling, and children laughing. The Whaley ghosts don't seem the least bit shy about showing themselves to visitors either; their faces suddenly appear in mirrors and on numerous photos taken in the house. The spirits seem so fond of letting in fresh air that the windows have all been permanently sealed, but the bedroom curtains still billow in breezes from a century ago. Even the beds appear to have been slept in, although the bedroom doorways are covered with panes of glass. In short, the Whaley House may be one of the most active haunted houses on earth.

Whaley House Museum is open September through May from 10:00 A.M. to 5:00 P.M. and June through August from 10:00 A.M. to 10:00 P.M. It is closed on Christmas Day. Groups larger than fifteen should call ahead for reservations. Entry fees apply.

NOB HILL INN
1000 Pine Street
San Francisco, CA 94109
(415) 673-6080
www.nobhillinn.com

By the dawn of the twentieth century, the Nob Hill district of San Francisco rivaled Chicago, Denver, and even New York for elegant architecture and wealthy residents, but all that came to a devastating end on April 18, 1906. An earthquake, estimated at 8.0 on the Richter scale, ripped the city apart. The gas lines left exposed by the quake quickly ignited and burned down most of the surviving buildings.

Within a year, the city was rebuilding. One of the elegant Edwardian houses that took the place of their Victorian predecessors was located at the corner of Pine and Taylor streets. Despite extensive research by later occupants, all evidence of the original owners of this building seems to have vanished. No matter who they were, it is obvious they wanted nothing but the best. Bubbling over with bay windows and turrets, the house now known as the Nob Hill Inn was a symbol that elegance had not deserted San Francisco. The house went through many changes of ownership through the decades, and like so many grand old places, its fortunes and physical condition slowly declined. In 1984, it changed hands again and was renovated and converted for use as an upscale hotel.

The renovation process seems to have stirred up a host of spirits, but they are anonymous, because none of them materialize into physical form. According to several psychics and ghost hunters, there may be as many as twenty-two spirits living here, many of them probably originating from that terrible day in 1906 and, therefore, actually predating the current structure. What we know with a greater degree of certainty is that all of them play the usual games with the living—moving small objects from place to place, unlocking and slamming doors, and playing merry havoc with electrical systems and electronic gadgets, such as cameras and cell phones.

Nob Hill Inn is open all year. In addition to overnight accommodations, the inn offers breakfast service and afternoon tea and sherry. While in San Francisco, take the Vampire Tour ghost tour; call (650) 279-1840 or visit www.sfvampiretour.com.

WINCHESTER MYSTERY HOUSE
525 S. Winchester Boulevard
San Jose, CA 95128
(408) 247-2101
www.winchestermysteryhouse.com

The deadly efficiency of the Winchester repeating rifle made a vast fortune for the Winchester family. When company founder Oliver Winchester died in 1880, control of the company and money went to his only son, William. William had already been married to Sarah Pardee for eighteen years when he inherited the family business, and during that time, they had only one child, Annie, who died at only a few weeks old. Sarah never quite recovered from her daughter's death, and when William died in 1881, one year after his father, Sarah fell apart. Seeking comfort from a psychic, Sarah was told that her family was cursed by the ghosts of everyone killed by her family's guns, and it was Sarah's duty to build a home for these restless spirits.

Consequently, Sarah moved to California, where she bought a piece of land in San Jose and began building and building and building. Construction on the ghost house continued until the day she died, thirty-eight years later. Virtually nothing in the house made any sense, at least to the living. With 1,257 windows, 950 doors (many of them leading nowhere) and forty staircases (some ending against blank walls), the Winchester House was designed only to accommodate, or possibly confuse, the deceased. Sarah alone inhabited the strange mansion, holding séances and chatting with her ghosts. The number of spirits that remain in the house, or how many ever did, is unknown, but the bizarre Winchester mansion is undoubtedly among the best-known haunted houses in the world.

Winchester Mystery House is open daily from 9:00 A.M. to 7:00 P.M. It is closed on Christmas Day. A variety of tours are available. Entry fees apply to all tours.

COLORADO

MOLLY BROWN HOUSE MUSEUM
1340 Pennsylvania Avenue
Denver, CO 80203
(303) 832-4092
www.mollybrown.org

The Unsinkable Molly Brown is remembered today for surviving the 1912 sinking of the *Titanic* and helping to organize the care of other survivors. In truth, the *Titanic* disaster must have seemed like small potatoes to the dynamic Brown. Her nearly forgotten husband, James, managed the Ibex Mining Company, located in ore-rich Leadville, Colorado, and he and Molly saved enough money to buy a site for James to open his own mine. The Little Johnny, as it was known, turned out to be Colorado's richest gold mine, bringing in 135 tons of high-grade ore every day during the height of its operation in 1893. The house the Browns bought in Denver was not a grand mansion, but it did boast electric lights, a telephone, indoor plumbing, and central heating. Determined to do the most good with her piles of cash, Molly promoted a juvenile justice system, got involved with the Red Cross, and a few years after surviving the sinking of the *Titanic*, went to France to work with American soldiers during World War I. By the time Molly died in 1932, her old home had fallen on hard times; by

1970, it was slated for demolition. Then Historic Denver stepped in, restored the house to its 1890s appearance, and opened it as a museum.

Since then, Molly, James, and at least three other former inhabitants have resumed residence. Molly appears at the dining room table and occasionally rearranges the chairs. The scent of James's cigars and pipe waft through the house, despite the fact that Molly never let him smoke inside while they were alive. Molly's mother, Johanna, is seen at the window of one of the bedrooms, where the blinds there go up and down of their own accord. A particularly unhappy butler has been spotted peering out of a mirror near the bottom of the stairs. Even the ghost of Molly's cat shows up here and there.

Molly Brown House Museum is open September through May from 10:00 A.M. to 3:30 P.M. on Tuesday through Saturday and 12:00 P.M. to 3:30 P.M. on Sunday. During June, July, and August the museum is also open on Monday from 10:00 A.M. to 3:30 P.M. Tours last about forty-five minutes. It is closed on legal holidays. Admission charges apply.

BLACK AMERICAN WEST MUSEUM
3091 California Street
Denver, CO 80205
(303) 482-2242
www.blackamericanwestmuseum.com

Dr. Justina Ford was truly an amazing woman. Born in 1871, she was one of America's first licensed female physicians and possibly its first licensed black female doctor. After graduating from medical school in 1899, she moved to Denver, and despite gender and racial prejudices, she remained in practice until shortly before her death in 1952. Although she delivered more than seven thousand babies, it was not until two years before she died that the Colorado Medical Society granted her membership.

Nearly twenty years after Ford died, her house became the Black American West Museum, and it seems that she was pleased enough with the transformation to make her presence known. A former pediatrician, Ford is known to appear to children only; when she does it is a full-bodied, solid apparition, with enough substance that she has actually led children around by the hand. She has introduced herself to the kids by her first name, and they have identified her from photographs.

Black American West Museum is open from September through May on Tuesday through Saturday from 10:00 A.M. to 2:00 P.M. and from June through August on Tuesday through Saturday from 10:00 A.M. to 5:00 P.M. It is closed on all legal holidays. Admission fees apply.

GRANT-HUMPHREYS MANSION
770 Pennsylvania Street
Denver, CO 80203
(303) 894-2505
www.coloradohistory.org/ghm/rentalsGrantHum.htm

James B. Grant was a mining engineer who made a sizeable fortune smelting down gold and silver ore. Never one to stint on the finer things in life, he built in Denver in 1902 one of the most extravagant houses the city had ever seen. With thirty rooms, twenty-foot-tall columns, terra-cotta balustrades, and projecting balconies, it looked much like a yellowbrick version of the White House in Washington, D.C. Grant died only nine years after finishing the house, and his widow sold it to Albert Humphreys, who soon died in a suspicious gun-related accident on the third floor.

It was not a house with particularly good vibes. Maybe this is because, up until a decade before it was built, the land had been occupied by Denver's Mount Prospect Cemetery, commonly known as Boot Hill. Between 1858 and 1893, a lot of good, honest people had been buried there, but so had a lot of gunslingers and criminals. In 1893, Denver ordered the cemetery to be moved within ninety days, so the city could sell the land for development. The Catholic and Jewish bodies were moved by their respective congregations, but most of the others were desecrated, dumped into random boxes, and robbed of personal possessions, with their bones left littering the ground only to be plowed under.

The mansion is currently used as city offices. The ghosts of Albert Humphreys, undoubtedly unhappy over his untimely and mysterious death, and at least four other unidentified spirits, believed to be from the old graveyard, still roam the halls and rooms of the house. Nearby Cheesman Park, which was also once part of the cemetery, is also considered to be notably haunted.

Grant-Humphreys Mansion is closed to the public, but it opens on special occasions, particularly in October, when lectures on ghosts and the paranormal are held. Check their Web site for specific dates and times.

ROSEMONT MUSEUM
419 W. 14th Street
Pueblo, CO 81003
(719) 545-5290
http://www.rosemount.org/home

John Thatcher was one of those individuals who had a gift for making money. After moving to Pueblo in 1863, he parlayed one successful small business into several more and used the profits to open Pueblo's first bank. In 1893, he spent an astonishing $60,000 on a wonderful twenty-four thousand-square-foot house, built of Colorado's native pink volcanic rock. He then set his wife to furnishing the place in the height of style. Rosemont, as the house was called, remained in the family for seventy-five years before becoming a museum in 1968.

No one knows if the ghostly entities were in the house when the Thatcher family owned it, or even who or how many spirits there are. Disembodied footsteps are heard in empty hallways, and numerous visitors catch fleeting glimpses of moving, shifting shapes and fleeting lights out of the corners of their eyes.

Rosemont Museum is open February through December, Tuesday through Saturday from 10:00 A.M. to 4:00 P.M. The museum is closed on major holidays and during January. An admission fee is charged. There is a restaurant on site.

HAWAII

IOLANI PALACE
364 South King St.
Honolulu, HI 96813
(808) 532-1051
www.iolanipalace.org

As the only official residence of a monarch inside the United States, Iolani Palace occupies a very special place in American history. Built in 1882 by King Kalakaua, the palace was the center of the Royal Hawaiian government, as well home to the king and his sister, Princess Liliu'okalani. Less than a decade after building this national showplace, Kalakaua fell ill, and on the advice of his physicians, he traveled to the drier climate of California, in hope of regaining his health. The attempt failed and in 1891 the king died in San Francisco. On his death, the crown of Hawaii passed to Liliu'okalani, who began to institute a series of reforms that displeased the rich American industrialists and plantation owners who owned large swaths of Hawaii. Backed by the American minister to Hawaii and three companies of U.S. marines and sailors, the American business interests mounted a coup against Queen Liliu'okalani, forcing her to abdicate. Adding insult to injury, the queen was put on trial and imprisoned in Iolani Palace, while her nation became nothing more than a U.S. colony.

No wonder then that the queen's sad, restless spirit still haunts the building where she once ruled and was later held prisoner. Late at night, palace guards often see inexplicable lights and shadows fleeting along the hallways. More eerie are the wet footprints in the hallways that begin out of nowhere, travel for some distance, and then just stop. Strangest of all is the figure of a young Hawaiian girl who walks up the stairs leading to a disused fountain on the palace grounds. Occasionally, around sunset, she ascends the stairs, wanders around the palace grounds weeping and wailing, and finally vanishes into thin air.

Iolani Palace is open Tuesday through Saturday from 9:00 A.M. to 5:00 P.M. and is closed Sunday, Monday, and national holidays. Admission fees apply. Oahu Ghost Tours offers a walking tour of haunted sites on Thursdays and Saturdays at 7:00 P.M. Visit their Web site at www.robertshawaii.com/oahu/honolulu-haunts-tour .php.

IDAHO

BJ'S BAYOU RESTAURANT
655 N. 2880 E
Roberts, ID 83444
(208) 228-2331

Like a lot of old structures, the building that now houses BJ's Bayou Restaurant has been many things over the one-hundred-and-twenty-plus years of its existence. Beginning life as Roberts's one and only fancy hotel, which included the town post office and barber shop, it has since served as a brothel, a hospital, and cheap apartments. In 1976, it was nearly wiped off the map by a disastrous flood that swept through Roberts. Subsequently, it stood abandoned and forlorn until the late 1980s, when it was purchased and renovated into a Cajun restaurant, with offices and living quarters for the owner and her family on the upper floors.

It didn't take long before the new owners heard the local gossip about the old building being haunted, but they never paid much attention. After all, every town has a haunted house story. During the renovation process, however, the owner, her family and workmen all started seeing some very strange visitors wandering around the empty halls and rooms of the old building. According to everyone who has witnessed the more than fifteen spirits who still inhabit BJ's, they appear just as solid and lifelike as real people. Although they are dressed in the clothing of the late nineteenth century and early twentieth century, and can walk through walls and closed doors, nearly all of BJ's revenants look like living people. Although primarily active after the restaurant is closed, they have occasionally been spotted making merry during business hours. The most frequent visitor is known as "Sam," and he seems endlessly fascinated with the dryer. He opens the door, pulls out clothes, and scatters them across the floor. At other times, Sam likes to hold doors open for people, at least until they get close, at which point he slams the door and disappears.

Other ghosts at BJ's include a Chinese cook, a maid, a young woman dressed in an evening gown, and a sinister-looking man in a black frock coat. Whether keeping to themselves or appearing in full view of customers, the ghosts go about their business, banging in and out of the swinging doors, breaking glasses, and making off with the silverware.

BJ's Bayou Restaurant is open Tuesday and Sunday from 4:00 P.M. to 9:00 P.M. and Wednesday and Thursday from 4:00 P.M. to 10:00 P.M. On Friday and Saturday, according to the manager, the restaurant stays open "till everybody leaves." BJ's is closed Mondays.

JAMESON SALOON AND INN
304 6th Street
Wallace, ID 83873
(208) 556-6000

The town of Wallace was founded in 1885 as the center of what would become a vast, and vastly profitable, silver-mining operation. Four years later, a forty-three-year-old entrepreneur named Ted Jameson moved to town and built a three-story hotel and restaurant to cater to the hoards of miners who were already flocking to Wallace in the hopes of making a quick fortune. Jameson himself never lived at his hotel, but more than a dozen resident prostitutes lived and worked out of Jameson's establishment. Predictably, life in and around the hotel's saloon and guest rooms was pretty rowdy, and much of the violence and gaiety that once filled the halls and rooms continues to linger in the form of a variety of spirit manifestations.

The Jameson's most famous spirit, and the only one specifically identified, is known as "Maggie." We don't know Maggie's last name, but a lot of nineteenth-century prostitutes preferred to keep their family names private. According to the story, Maggie fell in love with one of her regular customers, a miner who actually had the good fortune to strike it rich. The man told Maggie he had to take a quick trip back east, but that he would be back shortly and then they would marry and leave Wallace. Maggie believed him, and although her lover never returned, Maggie spent the remainder of her life living in Room 3 of the Jameson, pining for her unfaithful man. Today Maggie's ghost is often sighted in her old room as well as in other places in the Jameson. Guests who stay in Room 3 are routinely locked in, or out, of their room. Some visitors have reported seeing the image of a woman in nineteenth-century dress peering at them from the mirror and have even heard a disembodied woman's voice in the room late at night. Small objects are constantly moved from place to place. Staff and customers in the old saloon frequently hear people laughing and talking all over the room, even when there is no one there. Sometimes these voices last only for a few moments and at other times can go on for hours. On rare occasions the sound of a ghostly argument breaks out, followed by the sharp, deafeningly loud report of a gun being fired; then silence descends, at least until the next time the miners and cowboys become active.

Jameson Saloon and Inn has been fully restored to its 1889 appearance and is open all year. It operates as a bed-and-breakfast, restaurant, and bar. The restaurant and saloon are open to the public.

MONTANA

COPPER KING MANSION
219 W. Granite Street
Butte, MT 59701
(406) 782-7580
www.thecopperkingmansion.com

William Clark was an enterprising sort of guy. After completing law school he went west in 1862 to dig for gold. But digging with a long-handled shovel was not quite his thing, so after working his claim for two years and selling it for $1,500, he began selling supplies to miners. Then he became a claims recorder and loaned money to miners based on their mines' estimated worth. He also helped miners manage their money. By working on the edges of the mining industry, Clark amassed a fortune, which at its height was bringing in a tidy $17 million a month. Between 1884 and 1888, he took a meager one day's pay and built a $500,000, thirty-four-room mansion in Butte. This wasn't his only home, of course, but it was his favorite. The house was eventually inherited by his son, who gambled away all of his father's money and had to sell the house. For a while it served as a convent and then it was sold and resold. The mansion was finally rescued and turned into a stunning bed-and-breakfast.

The identities of those who haunt this fine old house are unknown, but one of them lives on the third floor where the old ballroom and the nun's chapel are located. He or she delights in startling visitors by moving objects around the room. The game-room emits a distinct feeling of coldness. An amorphous, hazy apparition floats through the basement and along the first-floor hallway. The owners of the Copper King Mansion, as the Clark house is known today, say there are no ghosts here, but numerous guests, visitors, and former staff members disagree.

Copper King Mansion is open daily April through September from 9:00 A.M. to 4:00 P.M. From October through March, tours are available by appointment only. Tours are free for overnight guests, otherwise entry fees apply.

HOTEL MEADE
Bannack State Park
4200 Bannack Road
P.O. Box 1426
Dillon, MT 59725
(406) 834-3413
www.bannack.org

Once upon a time Bannack was a thriving town; it was so thriving, in fact, that the local citizenry thought it should be chosen for the county seat. In preparation for the expected honor, the town built a courthouse in 1875. The county seat, however, was located in Dillon, twenty-five miles away, so the courthouse sat empty until 1881, when local physician John Singleton Meade bought the place and refitted it as a combination residence, hotel, community center, doctor's office, and as the need arose, hospital.

There were some deaths in the hospital area, but the most notable tragedy was the 1916 death of the daughter of Hotel Meade's manager. The teenage Dorothy Dunn was swimming in a local dredge pond with friends when she drowned. Since then, she has appeared in and around the hotel, usually manifesting herself to children. She is clear enough that her blue, turn-of-the-century dress is unmistakable. Although she apparently tries to speak, she seems unable to make any sound. The townsfolk of Bannack accepted Dorothy as part of the hotel's charm, but by World War II, Bannack's mines had played out and the charm of the whole town pretty much died after everyone left.

Today Bannack has a new kind of charm; it is one of America's best-preserved ghost towns, with about sixty standing buildings, including the Hotel Meade. Dorothy is still there, sometimes appearing in the second-floor window. Accompanying her are the spirits of other women from the town, who occasionally appear in the windows or float down the hotel's halls. The sounds of children crying have been heard in the building. On the second-floor stair landing, visitors are sometimes overwhelmed by strange feelings of disorientation. Cold spots are evident in the second-floor hall. The largest suite of rooms, located at the second-floor front, is permanently locked, reportedly because of intense paranormal activity. EVP recordings have been taken throughout the second floor.

Hotel Meade and the town of Bannack are part of Bannack State Park. The park is open daily, all year, during daylight hours. Admission is free.

BRANTLEY MANSION
Holter Street
Helena, MT 59601

Most middle- to upper-class people who lived during the nineteenth century were committed to the ideals of hard work and formal manners. Even by these rigid standards though, Montana supreme court judge Theodore Brantley was a stickler for decorum. He left his fine mansion every morning before his wife and children were up and returned late at night after they were in bed. Still, he cared for his family deeply, and on his way to his attic office he stopped at each family member's room to peek in and make sure everyone and everything was alright. Brantley passed away in 1922, but the big house remained in the family until 1970, when it was converted into luxury apartments.

The renovation process awakened the spirit of the good judge. As soon as the new owners moved into their top-floor apartment, they began hearing the strange sound of someone opening the front door, coming up the stairs, opening and closing every door in the house, and finally moving up to the attic room that Brantley used as his office. Another tenant noticed that any small candies left in a dish disappeared. No one has ever seen the judge, but even four decades after his first appearance, his nightly routine is still heard. As for the candy, suffice it to say that no one in the old Brantley Mansion ever leaves sweets in an open dish.

Brantley Mansion is not open to the public, so do not trespass on the property. Helena offers a ghost walk and tour that stops at the house. If you wish to see the Brantley Mansion, visit the Haunted Helena Ghost Walk Web site at www.goldwest.visitmt.com/listings/ 17337.htm or call (406) 422-5911. Tours are held every Tuesday, Friday, and Saturday at 8:00 P.M.

NEVADA

BLISS MANSION
608 Elizabeth Street
Carson City, NV 89703
(775) 887-8988
www.blissmansion.com

Duane Bliss was a man who liked to plan ahead. He began amassing his fortune by selling lumber to local mines, where it was used as pit props in the mine shafts. When business boomed, he diversified into railroads and construction, acting as general contractor for houses and buildings in Carson City, Lake Tahoe, and San Francisco. In 1860, he bought a prime piece of real estate in Carson City, where he planned to build his house. The fact that the land was occupied by a cemetery did not bother him in the least; he simply bought more land, moved the bodies, and by 1879, his house was finished. And a grand house it was, too. At the time of completion, Bliss's mansion was the only house in town with a telephone and gas lighting, and it was the largest private residence in all of Nevada. The Bliss family remained in the house for four generations. The old homestead was then sold and converted into a bed-and-breakfast.

The entire family never left, at least not in the spirit sense. Many visitors and several subsequent owners say Duane Bliss is still hanging around. He has appeared on several occasions both inside and outside the house, but he always stays long enough for the living to spot him before he vanishes into thin air. Whether

Bliss remains here because he loves his house or because he is being punished for disturbing the final resting places of those whose bodies he moved off his land is anybody's guess.

Bliss Mansion is a bed-and-breakfast inn that is open all year.

NEVADA GOVERNOR'S MANSION
606 N. Mountain Street
Carson City, NV 89703
(775) 882-2333

Nevada officially joined the Union in 1864, near the end of the Civil War, but it took the state legislature more than four decades to get around to building a mansion for the state's governor. In 1907, the state approved the logically named Mansion Bill, and two years later, Gov. Denver Dickerson and his family moved into their new, if temporary, home. Only two months later, the state's first lady, Una Dickerson, gave birth to a daughter named June—the first and only child ever to be born in the house.

There was no sign that the Nevada Governor's Mansion was haunted until the 1950s, when two female spirits, presumably a mother and her small daughter, were seen walking along the second-floor hallway. Later, the sound of a man's footsteps began emanating from the main staircase between the first and second floors. Although the entities have never been identified, one theory is that they are connected to an antique clock that came as a gift to the house in the 1950s, dragging the ghosts along with it. This makes sense, because the time frames of the clock's arrival and the appearance of the ghosts are in sync. In addition to the three spirits, the doors to the parlor sometimes open by themselves and a cold presence moves through the open door. The mother and daughter are thought by some to be First Lady Una Dickerson and her daughter June.

Nevada Governor's Mansion is open to the public one day per year only, on Nevada Day, which takes place on the last Saturday of October. Tours are free. For more information, contact the Carson City Convention and Visitor's Bureau at (775) 687-7410 or (800) 638-2321.

METRO SALON AND DAY SPA
121 California Avenue
Reno, NV 89509
(775) 786-8686

To those casually passing by, the former Levy house looks just a little bit odd and slightly out of place. Built in 1906 by a mining and mercantile magnate named William Levy, the house was grand enough, having all the neo-classical styling and appointments expected in a mansion of the period. At the time it probably didn't look strange at all—that came about later. In 1940, Levy died and his daughters, Mildred and Fritzi, divided the land the house sat on. Fritzi leased her half of the land to a gas station. Mildred kept the house, turned it ninety degrees, and moved it slightly to the west. That's why it looks odd; it isn't where it should be. After Mildred died, the house was subdivided and leased out to various businesses. Today, the Metro Salon and Day Spa is located on the ground floor of the house and private offices are on the upper floors. The current occupants seem to have gotten an equal share of the hauntings.

Who the entities are remains a mystery. There are at least five spirits haunting the old place. Three of them are children, all of whom live on the third floor and are around ten years of age. The sound of their running feet can be heard often in the rear area of the third-floor rooms. There are also the seldom-seen ghosts of a man in a black suit and a woman who limits herself to the basement area. The house experiences several cold spots—some of them are static and others are mobile—all confined to the second and third floors. Numerous visitors and employees have experienced unaccountable mood swings, fear, uneasiness, and splitting headaches in the attic, in the cellar, and on the staircase. The house has been investigated several times, and a number of disembodied voices have been recorded.

Metro Salon and Day Spa is open all year, Monday through Friday, from 9:00 A.M. to 8:00 P.M. and Saturday from 9:00 A.M. to 3:00 P.M. The upper floors are not open to the public.

MACKAY MANSION
129 S. D Street
P.O. Box 971
Virginia City, NV 89440
(775) 847-0336
www.mackaymansion.com

After being apprenticed as a shipbuilder in New York in the 1840s, John Mackay headed west to San Francisco to mine for gold. The backbreaking work was not what Mackay was looking for, so he followed the silver strikes to Virginia City, Nevada. Here he did not dig for silver, but employed his skill as a carpenter in and around the mines. With the money he earned, he invested in mining stock, and between 1866 and 1869, he bought controlling interest in four major mines, as well as the offices of one of his holdings, the Gould and Curry Mining Company. Built in 1859, the Gould and Curry offices formerly served as both mine office and home of George Hearst, chief shareholder of the mine. Mackay rebuilt and revamped the building into a grand home and lived there for nearly thirty years until his death in 1902 at the age of seventy. The house changed hands several times over the years and was put to a number of uses. In more recent years it has been transformed into an events center, catering to weddings and other affairs, and offering tours of how the rich and famous lived in the 1870s.

Adding to the richness of the Mackay Mansion's history are at least three unidentified ghosts. One is the well-formed spirit of a little girl wearing a white dress, who lingers in a second-floor room, which may have been her bedroom. Floating, glowing orbs, which have been photographed, also manifest in this room. Across the hall, visitors have heard the phantom child playing with her toys. Another ghost with limited range is that of an elderly man affectionately known as "the Colonel," who lives in the kitchen. Sometimes he is seen sitting at the table and sometimes in the old rocking chair, but he never leaves the room. In contrast to these relatively sedentary spirits is the woman in Victorian-era clothing who makes endless trips up and down the big staircase, sometimes relaxing for a moment in a high-backed chair in the living room, before returning to her endless round of work.

Mackay Mansion is open for tours all year, during regular business hours, but you must email ahead to make arrangements. Entry fees apply.

GOLD HILL HOTEL
Highway 342
P.O. Box 740
Virginia City, NV 89440
(775) 847-0111
www.goldhillhotel.net

During the boom days of the Comstock Lode, Virginia City needed all the hotels and lodging houses it could get. The building now known as the Gold Hill Hotel was originally built in 1859 by the Riesen family as a private home with rooms to rent to miners and travelers. By 1862, the house had changed hands, become a full-time hotel, and had an extension added to one side that contained a restaurant and saloon. Over the last century and a half, the building changed hands and uses many times and has been renovated nearly as often.

The continual and rapid turnover of guests makes it impossible to identify the ghosts who call this hotel home, but the locations of their individual haunts are well-defined. Room 4 is referred to as Rosie's Room, because the spirit who resides there is always accompanied by the strong scent of roses. Tradition says she may have been one of the working girls who once offered her services to the miners. Whatever her background, she exhibits a sense of humor. She turns the lights on and off at all hours and enjoys hiding small objects and personal belongings, sometimes making them disappear for some time before returning them to the exact spot where they should have been all along. Nearby, in Room 5, an entity known as William is believed to be one of thirty-seven miners who died in a mineshaft fire in 1873 at the nearby Yellowjacket Mine. The scent of his tobacco is often reported in the room, and he has the frustrating habit of locking hotel guests out of his room. His muttering voice and footsteps have also been heard in the room, his face has been seen in the mirror, and on several occasions, guests have been awakened when their bed shakes violently. Then there are the children. They don't have individual identities, but the sound of their running feet and playful laughter can be heard moving back and forth along the second-floor hallway.

Gold Hill Hotel is open all year. It offers rooms and a full-service restaurant and bar, as well as a dinner theater during autumn months.

NEW MEXICO

ST. JAMES HOTEL
17 Collinson Street
Cimarron, NM 87714
(575) 376-2664

When Abraham Lincoln was murdered in April 1865, his chef, Henry Lambert, assumed he was out of a job. Henry went west, eventually landed in the cow town of Cimarron, and in 1872, opened a small restaurant with ample living quarters for himself and his wife. By 1880, Lambert's restaurant had become so popular that he added thirty guest rooms. As one of the few professional chefs between the Mississippi River and San Francisco, he quickly attracted a clientele that included every noteworthy Western character on both sides of the law, including Jesse James (who always stayed in Room 14), Bob Ford, Billy the Kid, Pat Garrett, and Kit Carson. Lew Wallace wrote part of his epic novel *Ben Hur* here. The Earp brothers and Doc Holliday stayed here on their way to Tombstone. Buffalo Bill Cody and Annie Oakley laid plans for the Wild West Show in the saloon. In the saloon alone there were twenty-six murders, and that doesn't include the forty-three more that took place in the rooms and restaurant. The gunfire was so furious that in 1901 more than four hundred bullet holes in the roof were repaired. Twenty-two still remain in the dining room ceiling.

One of the notable deaths, which lead to one of the St. James's hauntings, was that of T. J. Wright, who was shot in the back while returning to Room 18 after winning big at poker. Still angry at not collecting his winnings, Wright haunts the room so frequently that it is permanently locked. Across the hall, Room 17 contains the ghost of Lambert's wife, Mary, whose perfume often scents the air; her shadowy ghost haunts the hall outside as well. The entire second floor is often filled with cigar smoke. Elsewhere, electrical appliances refuse to work, long-dead faces materialize in the mirror behind the bar, and doors open and close by themselves. Unidentified groups of cowboys appear in the old saloon or play endless games of poker on the second floor.

St. James Hotel is open all year.

THE LODGE RESORT AND SPA
1 Corona Place
Cloudcroft, NM 88317
(575) 682-2566
www.thelodgeresort.com

The Lodge was built in 1899 as a residence for lumber company officials and lumberjacks who provided ties for the growing railroad. It was such a nice place, providing such a nice view at nine thousand feet above sea level, that in 1906 it was opened as a public hotel. Largely rebuilt after a fire in 1911, it became a fashionable haunt for the famous and infamous. Francisco "Pancho" Villa, Clark Gable, and Judy Garland all stayed here during the 1920s and 1930s when The Lodge served as a speakeasy, gambling den, and part-time brothel. One of the waitresses at this time, who reportedly served her customers more than food and drink, was known only as Rebecca. She had an ongoing affair with a local lumberjack who became enraged when he discovered she was seeing other men. One thing led to another and the lumberjack murdered Rebecca. Neither she nor the lumberjack has left the site of their final encounter.

Rebecca's ghost has been adopted by The Lodge. Her photos hang throughout the building, and her image has been immortalized in a stained-glass window. Not that anyone needs to be reminded what she looked like. Rebecca still makes very regular appearances. Her startlingly beautiful and lifelike apparition, replete with flaming red hair and sparkling blue eyes, is often seen moving along the halls, sometimes pausing to rearrange the bouquets. She also appears as a reflection in the back-bar mirror, on the dance floor dancing alone after hours, and in the bathtubs of startled guests. Even when she is invisible, she makes her presence known. Small objects float through the air, empty glasses explode on the tables, and lights go on and off. At least once, a pile of very real 1930s-era poker chips suddenly materialized in the middle of the barroom floor. Her erstwhile lover is here, too. Female guests have reported being awakened in the middle of the night by a cold hand on their shoulder and a ghostly voice whispering, "Won't you be my true love?"

The Lodge Resort and Spa is open all year and its full-service restaurant and bar are open to the public.

OLD CUCHILLO BAR
Highway 52
Cuchillo, NM 87901
(575) 743-2296
www.cuchillobar.com

At 180 years of age, this former dual-purpose home and stagecoach stop is built from adobe bricks, comprised of nothing more than mud and straw. It is impressive if only because it has survived so long. Over the years, the Old Cuchillo has been used as a private home, special occasion rental hall, trading post, post office, general store, and saloon. Somewhere along the way it also seems to have picked up at least one unidentified spectral resident.

The most common phenomenon is the sound of someone loading wood into a potbellied stove. The door opens, the wood is thrown in, and the door closes, despite the fact that the old stove has long since gone out of use. Mysterious whispers are also heard, the TV turns on and off by itself, cupboards open and close on their own, and bottles and other objects fly off the old saloon shelves. Even the current owner considers the place so haunted that he refuses to go inside after he closes the bar. Not much goes on in Cuchillo these days. The town has shrunk from two thousand to just thirty-five people. If you are traveling near the town of Truth or Consequences and feel like enjoying a few spirits, either out of the bottle or out of the past, stop at the Old Cuchillo Bar only twelve miles northwest of town.

Old Cuchillo Bar is open all year.

LA POSADA DE SANTA FE RESORT AND SPA

330 E. Palace Avenue
Santa Fe, NM 87501
(575) 986-0000 or (866) 331-7625
http://laposada.rockresorts.com

By the end of the Civil War, Abraham Staab had made a tidy fortune supplying goods and materials to the Union government. At the end of the war, he and his wife Julia moved west, where there was endless opportunity and little competition. Settling in Santa Fe, they built a grand Second Empire house with a massive ballroom tucked under the third-floor mansard roof. They entertained, had six healthy children, and generally enjoyed life, until the early 1890s when Julia suffered a miscarriage with their seventh child. Following several more unsuccessful pregnancies, Julia fell into a deep depression, locked herself in her room, and died in 1896 at the age of fifty-two. A few years later, a fire swept through the third floor, destroying the ballroom. In 1913, Abraham Staab died a very rich, but unhappy, man. By the 1930s, the Staab mansion had become a hotel, which the owners called La Posada, Spanish for "inn." The old Staab estate remained a resort, and in the 1990s, it was purchased, refurbished, and expanded by the Rock Resort chain. By then, however, Julia Staab had already been back in residence for nearly twenty years.

Under the new management, the second floor of the main house is no longer used for guest rooms, but Julia's old room, more recently called Room 256, had often been visited by its former mistress. She particularly likes to draw a bath in the middle of the night, disturbing the sleeping guests in the process. At other times, she has been seen staring into her old room from outside the windows and sweeping majestically up the grand staircase between the first and second floors. In the bar and restaurant on the main floor, she has been seen calmly sitting in one of the chairs, dressed in full Victorian finery, and standing by one of the fireplaces. On several occasions, glasses on the back bar have inexplicably fallen off their shelves, one after another, in measured succession. There are also reported cold spots at some of Julia's favorite locations.

La Posada de Santa Fe Resort and Spa is open all year. Their full-service restaurant is open to the public.

OREGON

THE CHATEAU AT THE OREGON CAVES
20000 Caves Highway
Cave Junction, OR 97523
(877) 245-9022
http://ivcdo.projecta.com/sectionindex.asp?sectionid=2

When local contractor Gust Lium built his combination home-hotel-restaurant in 1934, he produced an architectural gem worthy of the great Frank Lloyd Wright. Straddling the walls of a steep canyon and the river beneath, Lium's rustic chateau stands six stories high and has a man-made river running through the middle of the third floor. From this point on things become a bit murky, because this is one of those cases where fact has become so mixed with legend that they have become nearly inseparable.

Whatever the truth, there seems little doubt that someone is haunting this wonderful building.

According to the story, only three years after Lium opened his chateau, a newlywed couple, Elizabeth and Oscar Smith, were registered to spend their honeymoon here. Evidently Elizabeth caught her husband flirting, or possibly worse, with one of the maids. In a fit of angry despair, she committed suicide in Room 310. How she ended her life is open to dispute. Some say she jumped from the window into the rocky gorge below; others say she slit her wrists in the bathtub. Still others insist she hanged herself from the heat pipe. Whatever the case, Elizabeth has never been able to leave the chateau. She still inhabits her old room, at least until it is rented out. When Room 310 is booked Elizabeth wanders the third-floor hall, moaning and weeping, sometimes taking up residence in the linen closet. Unhappy to be put out of her room even temporarily, she has been known to repack an arriving guest's luggage as a hint they should leave. Even when no one is staying in Room 310, Elizabeth is sometimes active, re-arranging the furniture or pushing it out into the hallway. The baby grand piano in the lobby has been known to play by itself, so evidently Elizabeth has musical talent or she has an unidentified companion inhabiting her little corner of the afterlife.

The Chateau at the Oregon Caves is open from May 1 through October 15. The restaurant is open for dinner from 6:00 P.M. to 8:00 P.M. Reservations for both the hotel and restaurant are recommended.

MCLOUGHLIN HOUSE
McLoughlin Memorial Association
713 Center Street
Oregon City, OR 97045
(503) 656-5146
www.mcloughlinhouse.org

Dr. John McLoughlin, a physician and CEO of the British-owned Hudson's Bay Company, founded Oregon City in 1842. Three years later, he and his wife Marguerite built a large, two-story house, where they lived for the rest of their lives. By the end of 1857, both of the McLoughlins had died, and their house became a fine hotel. Over the years, it served as a dormitory for woolen-mill workers, a brothel, cheap apartments, and finally a flophouse. In 1909, the house was rescued and moved to its present location in an open-air museum complex, where it is situated next to a house built in 1849 that once belonged to Dr. Forbes Barclay.

The hauntings did not begin until the 1970s, when the graves of John and Marguerite McLoughlin were moved from their original location to a site between the house's new location and the Barclay house. Since then both McLoughlins have made regular appearances in their home. John is usually seen as a shadow, moving along the upstairs hall from his old bedroom, down the stairs, and into the dining room. How do we know it is John? The shadow is six-and-a-half-feet tall, the same height as the good doctor. He has also been seen sitting on his bed and rocking in his bedroom rocking chair. Both John and Marguerite smoked, and the smell of his cigars and her pipe sometimes follows people through the house. Some people also smell freshly brewed coffee. Marguerite has been seen going up the main staircase in an evening gown.

Then there are the visitors from the Barclay house next door. Most frequently seen is a startlingly corporeal red-haired boy, between six and eight years old, who comes to visit with his ghostly dog. The dog has left muddy paw prints all over the McLoughlins' carpet, and living dogs refuse to enter the downstairs room arranged to look like John's office. The boy comes to take a nap in a former child's room, where the bedclothes are often rumpled. He also plays with the old toys, now locked in a display case, which have been seen to move on their own. A tea set may be similarly rearranged by Marguerite. The sounds of knocking on the walls are harpsichord music can be heard.

McLoughlin House is open all year, Wednesday through Saturday from 10:00 A.M. to 4:00 P.M. and Sunday 1:00 P.M. to 4:00 P.M. It is closed on major holidays. Admission is free.

WHITE EAGLE SALOON
836 N. Russell Street
Portland, OR 97227
(503) 282-6810
www.mcmenamins.com/index.php?loc=55

The area surrounding Portland's docks was less than savory during the early years of the twentieth century. Dockyards, railroad yards, filthy factories, and thousands of immigrants all crowded together in surroundings little better than tenement ghettos. In 1905, two Polish immigrants, Barney Soboleski and William Hryszko, pooled their resources and put up a building in the neighborhood that served as both their home and place of business. The main floor was a saloon, the upstairs was both their home and a white brothel, and the basement was reserved for Chinese and black prostitutes. Like so many places teeming with immigrants, not all of the girls were willing participants; many were abducted and held as virtual slaves. Some of the customers suffered a reverse fate, being drugged and hauled through a labyrinth of tunnels, and then sold to passing ships as forced labor. Violence at the White Eagle was so common that the bar earned the nickname "Bucket of Blood," and this violence led to at least one of the ghosts who still haunt the place.

A customer became enamored with one of the girls, known only as Rose, and offered to marry her. Fearful of reprisals from the management, she refused. Enraged, her lover stabbed her to death and she remains trapped on the second floor where she once worked. Doors to the second-floor rooms are known to slam open and shut simultaneously. The wailing of a female emanates from one of the rooms. A less distressed spirit is that of Barney, a former employee who worked at the White Eagle until his death in 1955. His ghost has been seen going down the basement stairs and peering from a second-floor window. The basement office is also the scene of some odd manifestations. Strange noises and indecipherable voices are common. On at least one occasion, a rain of old coins fell out of thin air. In the ladies' bathroom, rolls of toilet paper have floated through the air and unrolled. Today, the White Eagle is far more respectable; it is a popular venue for blues and jazz, but still the manifestations continue.

White Eagle Saloon is open all year, Monday through Thursday from 11:00 A.M. to 1:00 A.M., Friday and Saturday from 12:00 P.M. to 2:30 A.M., and Sunday from 4:00 P.M. to 11:00 P.M. Some of the haunted rooms on the second floor have been renovated and are available to overnight guests.

HECETA HEAD LIGHT KEEPER'S HOUSE
Heceta Head Lighthouse
92072 Highway 101 South
Yachats, OR 97498
(866) 547-3696
www.hecetalighthouse.com

There is nothing like a little restoration work to stir up a dormant spirit, and although the ghostly lady of the Heceta Head Lighthouse cottage has been around at least since the 1950s, she has been much more active since the house was restored in the 1970s. The lighthouse, along with the duplex cottage built for its keepers, was built between 1892 and 1894, and from then until the lighthouse went dark in 1963, a long succession of keepers and their families lived in the twin cottages.

The most likely candidate for the apparition known as the "Gray Lady" is Rue DeRay, wife of early-twentieth-century lighthouse keeper Frank DeRay. She was evidently a bit stern and domineering, but even in death she continues to mourn the loss of her infant child whose grave is located on the grounds. During the 1950s, Rue's mistlike form was occasionally seen and her grief-stricken cries and footsteps on the basement stairs were heard. Locked kitchen cupboards opened by themselves. Then the cottage was restored, and Rue began assuming a more defined, lifelike shape. Her skirt moves along the hallway and through a locked door, and her fully formed ghost moves into the kitchen. She seemed to take a particular delight in scaring the restoration carpenters by floating a few inches above the floor to scowl at them while they were working in the attic. She still likes to stare down at visitors from the attic windows. Unlike some ghosts, Rue actually prefers daylight appearances. Although she appears only occasionally, she is in full form, with gray hair, gray blouse, and gray skirt.

Heceta Head Light Keeper's House is now a bed-and-breakfast and interpretive center for the nearby lighthouse. It is open all year; regular tours of the house are given Memorial Day weekend through Labor Day, Thursday through Monday from 12:00 P.M. to 5:00 P.M. Advance reservations are highly recommended. To arrange a tour beyond the regular season, call (866) 547-3696. Tours are free but there is a fee for parking.

UTAH

MARY FIELDING SMITH HOUSE
This Is the Place Heritage Park
2601 E. Sunnyside Avenue
Salt Lake City, UT 84108
(801) 582-1847
www.thisistheplace.org

Hyrum Smith, along with his brother Joseph, founded the Church of Jesus Christ of Latter-Day Saints (the Mormons) in New York. The brothers set up outposts further west, but the founding of a new religion did not sit well with their neighbors, forcing the Mormons to flee from place to place. Along with the brothers came their families, including Hyrum's second wife, Mary, and their eight children. In 1844, the brothers and two followers were arrested in Illinois on charges of riot and treason. While awaiting trial, the jail was attacked by a mob, and Hyrum and Joseph were shot to death. Mary and the children refused to be deterred from their faith, eventually traveling with church elder Brigham Young to the Mormons' new home in what is now Salt Lake City. There Mary lived and died in a small cottage, which many years later was rescued and relocated to a living history museum area now known as This Is the Place Heritage Park.

One would think that Mary would have been happy that her old homestead was saved, yet something seems to make her unhappy. For decades now she has been seen standing in the doorway of the cabin shaking her finger angrily at people passing by. Volunteers at the park frequently say they hear her old clock chiming, but the clock has been absent from the house for many years.

This Is the Place Heritage Park is open daily all year from 9:00 A.M. to 5:00 P.M. It is closed on legal holidays. Entry fees apply.

BRIGHAM YOUNG FARMHOUSE
This Is the Place Heritage Park
2601 E. Sunnyside Avenue
Salt Lake City, UT 84108
(801) 582-1847
www.thisistheplace.org

Following the murders of brothers Joseph and Hyrum Smith, leadership of the Church of Jesus Christ of Latter-Day Saints (the Mormons) fell to elder Brigham Young. The story of Young leading his people across the inhospitable American West to their new home in what is now Salt Lake City is legendary. Less well-known is Young's experimental farm, where he tested to find which crops were best suited to the blistering heat of the desert. In a lovely Gothic Revival house that he called Forest Farm, Young installed several of his twenty-six wives and an ample number of laborers to assist with the work.

In the 1970s, a century after Young's death, the old farmhouse was bought and privately restored by a couple who insisted they saw Young, still as a bearded man in his 70s with a walking stick, and that he advised them on the restoration. After fifteen years of living with Young's phantom, the family donated the house to the Deseret Village Historical Park. At the handover reception, the couple chatted amiably with a young man dressed in 1880s clothes and had their picture taken with him. Startlingly, the final photo showed the man and his wife and only a gap where the young man had stood. The man had apparently been John Young, Brigham's son, and despite being dead for more than half a century, he appeared as real as anyone.

Since the house's relocation to what is today This Is the Place Heritage Park, the hauntings have continued unabated. Brigham himself occasionally pops up, as does his son John. The most frequent specter, however, is Brigham Young's nineteenth wife, Ann Eliza, a diminutive firecracker of a woman who divorced Young and now seems set on making his afterlife miserable. Young's second wife, Sara, also appears occasionally, as do an indeterminate number of his endless flock of children. The children are most often heard playing, singing, and dancing in the big second-floor room, once called the Ballroom, but which was actually a play area. Objects in the house have occasionally been known to float through the air, the smell of chicken soup and frying potatoes wafts from the kitchen, doorknobs rattle, and footsteps are heard throughout the house. Staff and docents once denied their ghosts, but today they seem rather proud of them.

This Is the Place Heritage Park is open daily all year from 9:00 A.M. to 5:00 P.M. It is closed on legal holidays. Entry fees apply.

MCCUNE MANSION
200 North Main Street
Salt Lake City, UT 84103
(801) 531-8866
www.mccunemansion.com

Alfred and Elizabeth McCune's former home looks like something out of a fairy tale—towers, turrets, shingles, and wraparound porches jutting out in every direction. McCune obviously had a lot of money; in 1900, he laid down no less than a half-million dollars to build his three-story, twenty-one-room house. The money came from McCune's investments in mining and railroads, and he was evidently good at what he did, because he attracted men like

J. P. Morgan, William Randolph Hearst, and Frederick Vanderbilt as business partners. By 1920, the McCunes no longer needed their big house, so they donated it to the Mormon Church. Over the next seventy years, the house changed hands at least three times before being bought and restored as a special function facility. Long before then, however, strange things had begun to happen.

In the 1950s, the sounds of music and voices were often heard by people passing by long after the house was closed for the day. During the daylight hours, doors unlocked, opened, closed, and relocked of their own accord. There were cold spots, and lights in various parts of the house went on and off without the aid of living hands. Today, two ghosts, both fully formed and solid, appear. One is the specter of a man, elegantly dressed in evening clothes and cape, who appears only when a single person is in the room. The other apparition is that of a girl about twelve years old with blond hair, who steps out of a long mirror hanging on one wall of the house's main floor. She often appears during weddings and other social functions held in the house. Photographed several times, she has also been known to walk from room to room and rearrange furniture and small items.

McCune Mansion is open for group tours of ten to twenty-five people by appointment only. Call at least two weeks in advance to make arrangements. Entry fees apply.

WASHINGTON

STANWOOD HOTEL AND SALOON
26926 102nd Ave N.W.
Stanwood, WA 98292
(360) 629-2888
www.stanwoodhotelandsaloon.com

Looking much like it did when it was built at the end of the 1890s, the Stanwood Hotel no longer serves as the home of its owner as it did when it was built. It still serves drinks across the old bar, provides lodgings for weary travelers, and offers entertainment for the bored and restless. Some of the restless spirits who have come here to be entertained over the years have been so pleased with the service that even the loss of mortal life has not induced them to leave.

One of the early attractions of the hotel was undoubtedly its part-time use of the second floor as a bordello, and some of the girls still seem anxious to service today's clientele. One of the more frequent, if invisible, spirits is a prostitute who is in the habit of walking up behind male customers seated at the bar and rubbing her chest against their backs. The most visible apparition is that of an early owner known only as "Marshall." Dressed in black trousers, vest, and old-fashioned sleeve garters, he has been seen at one of the tables intently playing solitaire with a deck of cards as insubstantial as he is. Witnesses have reported seeing the mustachioed Marshall elsewhere in the building, along with an unknown female apparition in early-twentieth-century clothing. One of the pair sometimes has been caught on security cameras as a mist that floats behind the bar.

The second floor offers a host of phenomena, including disembodied footsteps and indefinable odors; in Room 9, people report feeling extremely uncomfortable and hearing whispers and rapping noises. In the ground floor ladies toilet, people hear a man whistling. In nearly every room in the hotel, ghost hunters have taken recordings of disembodied voices, including one regular customer from the 1970s who has clearly identified himself as Charlie Howell Gibbons.

Stanwood Hotel and Saloon is open all year. As of this writing the overnight rooms were in the process of being remodeled; check their Web site for updates.

WYOMING

FERRIS MANSION BED AND BREAKFAST
607 W. Maple Street
Rawlins, WY 82301
(307) 324-3961

By the close of the nineteenth century, George Ferris had already made a small fortune out of his mining activities in and around Rawlins. The Ferris-Haggarty mine had long been one of the most prolific and profitable copper mines in Wyoming's history. Ferris parlayed his business savvy into large-scale social success in the form of political power. Twice in the 1870s, he was elected to the Wyoming Territorial Legislature, and he was chosen to be a delegate to the territory's Constitutional Convention when Wyoming vied for statehood.

By 1899, Ferris was the sole owner of his mine and had largely retired from public life. Deciding to enjoy his remaining years, and his money, he hired an architectural firm from Knoxville, Tennessee, to design the finest house Rawlins had ever seen. The result of their efforts was a spectacular Queen Anne mansion, but between the time ground was broken in late 1899 and its completion in 1903, tragedy had nearly destroyed the Ferris family.

Only weeks after construction on the mansion began, the youngest son, seven-year-old Cecil, was accidentally shot to death by his older brother while they played with one of their father's guns. The following year, Ferris himself died in a buggy accident near his mine. Before construction of the house was completed, two workmen died in on-site accidents. By the time the house was ready to be occupied, Julia Ferris and her surviving children were left to live there alone. The Ferris children eventually grew up and moved away, leaving Julia alone in the grand house until her death in 1931.

The Ferris home went through many incarnations before being restored and turned into a fine bed-and-breakfast inn, but from the time of Julia's death, there were always rumors that something was not quite right about the old place. For the past eight decades there have been constant electrical anomalies, reports of small objects mysteriously moving in full view of some startled person, and unidentifiable sounds permeating the house. Strangest of all are the apparitions of young Cecil Ferris and a woman in a long, flowing nightgown who is assumed to be Julia. More than one guest at the Ferris Mansion Bed and Breakfast has run from their room in panic when a small object on their dresser or bathroom sink has suddenly floated into the air of its own accord.

Ferris Mansion Bed and Breakfast is open all year. Reservations are required.

TRAIL END HISTORIC SITE
400 Clarendon Ave
Sheridan, WY 82801
(307)674-4589
www.trailend.org

Sheridan may have only twenty-eight thousand inhabitants, but it boasts the largest and most elaborate house museum in the state. Now called Trail End Historic Site, the old Sheridan mansion exemplifies the opportunities that awaited those willing to brave the hazards of the Old West.

When John Kendrick first came to Wyoming in 1879, he was a penniless twenty-one-year-old cowboy working on the first cattle drive organized by his future father-in-law, Charles Wulfjen. Twelve years later Kendrick married eighteen-year-old Eula Wulfjen over her father's protests, and the pair started a small cattle ranch of their own in Montana.

In 1910, the Kendricks moved to Sheridan, and John bought another ranch, expanded into politics, and was promptly elected to the state senate. Six years later, he had served as Wyoming's governor, was elected to the U.S. Senate, and owned a number of commercial buildings in downtown Sheridan. By 1913, the Kendricks had shelled out a whopping $165,000 to build a massive 13,700-square-foot mansion in the Flemish Revival style and surrounded it with nearly four acres of manicured gardens. Wyoming had never quite seen the like of the Kendricks' home. After John died in 1933, his widow moved out of the huge family home. In 1982, the house, along with many of the original furnishings, was donated to the state, which opened it as a museum.

No one seems to know exactly when the peculiar manifestations began, or who the ghosts might be, but there have been reports of strange happenings in the house since it became accessible to the public. Visitors often report feeling uncomfortable, sometimes to the point of panic, when they enter the kitchen and a Kendrick daughter's room. More mysterious is the phantom that enjoys following the security guard through the house on his nightly rounds. The guard has no reason to suspect that he is not alone in the house, but the video monitors consistently record images of a shadowy human form flitting from room to room, sometimes occupying the same room as the guard.

Trail End Historic Site is open seven days a week from March 1 through December 14. From March 1 through May 31, hours are 1:00 P.M. to 4:00 P.M. From June 1 through August 31, hours are 9:00 A.M. to 6:00 P.M. From September 1 through December 14, hours are 1:00 P.M. to 4:00 P.M. The site is closed Labor Day weekend, Veterans Day, Thanksgiving, and from December 15 through February 28. Admission fees apply.

STATE INDEX

Alabama
Drish Mansion, Tuscaloosa, 63
Gaineswood, Demopolis, 61
Sturdivant Hall, Selma, 62
Victoria, The, Anniston, 61

Alaska
Jesse Lee Home, Seward, 177

Arizona
Buford House Bed and Breakfast,
  Tombstone, 181
Casey Moore's Oyster House, Tempe, 180
Oliver House Bed and Breakfast, Bisbee,
  178
Riordan Mansion State Historic Park,
  Flagstaff, 179

Arkansas
Peel Mansion Museum and Garden,
  Bentonville, 65
Vino's Brewpub, Little Rock, 66

California
James Stuart Cain House, Bodie, 182
Madrona Manor Wine Country Inn and
  Restaurant, Healdsburg, 183
Nob Hill Inn, San Francisco, 186
Stokes Restaurant and Bar, Monterey, 183
Whaley House Museum, San Diego, 185
Winchester Mystery House, San Jose, 187

Colorado
Black American West Museum, Denver,
  189
Grant-Humphreys Mansion, Denver, 190
Molly Brown House Museum, Denver, 188
Rosemont Museum, Pueblo, 191

Connecticut
Benton House Museum, Tolland, 9
Lighthouse Inn, New London, 7
Monte Cristo Cottage Museum, New
  London, 8
Noah Webster House, West Hartford, 10
Talcott House Bed and Breakfast,
  Westbrook, 10

Delaware
Amstel House, New Castle, 12
Bellevue Hall, Wilmington, 13
Woodburn, the Home of Delaware's
  Governor, Dover, 11

District of Columbia
Octagon Museum, Washington, 14
White House, The, Washington, 15

Florida
Artist House, The, Key West, 68
Ernest Hemingway Home and Museum,
  Key West, 69
Herlong Mansion Historic Inn and
  Gardens, Micanopy, 70
Hernando Heritage Museum, Brooksville,
  67

Georgia
Hay House, Macon, 72
Juliette Gordon Low Birthplace, Savannah,
  75
Kehoe House, Savannah, 74
Olde Pink House Restaurant, Savannah, 73
Warren House, Jonesboro, 71

Hawaii
Iolani Palace, Honolulu, 192

Idaho
BJ's Bayou Restaurant, Roberts, 193
Jameson Saloon and Inn, Wallace, 194

Illinois
Beverly Unitarian Church, Chicago, 125
Culver House, Decatur, 127
Glessner House Museum, Chicago, 126
Old Slave House Museum, Junction, 128
Voorhies Castle, Bement, 129

Indiana
Hacienda Mexican Restaurant,
  Mishawaka, 132
Hannah House, Indianapolis, 131
Old Sheriff's House and Jail, Crown Point,
  130

STATE INDEX

Iowa
Brucemore, Cedar Rapids, 133
Mathias Ham House, Dubuque, 134
Villisca Ax Murder House, Villisca, 135

Kansas
Brown Mansion, Coffeyville, 137
Sauer Castle, Kansas City, 138
Strawberry Hill Museum, Kansas City, 139
Tuck U Inn at Glick Mansion, Atchison, 136

Kentucky
Ashland, the Henry Clay Estate, Lexington, 77
DuPont Mansion Bed and Breakfast, Louisville, 79
Liberty Hall Historic Site, Frankfort, 76
Loudon House, Lexington, 78
Southgate House, Newport, 80

Louisiana
Beauregard-Keyes House, New Orleans, 82
Columns Hotel, New Orleans, 83
Lalarie House, New Orleans, 84
Myrtles Plantation, St. Francisville, 85
T'Freres Bed and Breakfast, Lafayette, 81

Maine
Captain Fairfield Inn, Kennebunkport, 18
Captain Lord Mansion, Kennebunkport, 19
Kennebunk Inn, Kennebunk, 17

Maryland
Hampton National Historic Site, Towson, 23
Middleton Tavern, Annapolis, 20
Schifferstadt Architectural Museum, Frederick, 22
Surratt House Museum, Clinton, 21

Massachusetts
Hammond Castle Museum, Gloucester, 28
Higginson Book Company, Salem, 26
Lizzie Borden Bed and Breakfast/Museum, Fall River, 25
Porter-Phelps-Huntington Museum, Hadley, 24

Michigan
Bowers Harbor Inn, Traverse City, 142
Felt Estate, Holland, 140

National House Inn Bed and Breakfast, Marshall, 141

Minnesota
Forepaugh's Restaurant, St. Paul, 146
Gibbs Museum of Pioneer and Dakotah Life, St. Paul, 147
Glensheen, the Historic Congdon Estate, Duluth, 143
LeDuc Historic Estate, Hastings, 145

Mississippi
Cedar Grove Mansion Inn and Restaurant, Vicksburg, 88
Errolton, Columbus, 87
McRaven Tour Home, Vicksburg, 89
Waverly Mansion, West Point, 90

Missouri
Harry S. Truman National Historic Site, Independence, 148
James Farm, Kearney, 149
La Maison Guibourd-Valle, St. Genevieve, 150
Lemp Mansion, St. Louis, 151

Montana
Brantley Mansion, Helena, 198
Copper King Mansion, Butte, 196
Hotel Meade, Bannack State Park, 197

Nebraska
Brownville Historical Society, Brownville, 153
Fort Sidney Museum and Post Commander's Home, Sidney, 154
Ogallala Mansion on the Hill, Ogallala, 155

Nevada
Bliss Mansion, Carson City, 199
Gold Hill Hotel, Virginia City, 203
Mackay Mansion, Virginia City, 202
Metro Salon and Day Spa, Reno, 201
Nevada Governor's Mansion, Carson City, 200

New Hampshire
Country Tavern Restaurant and Pub, Nashua, 30
Mount Washington Resort, Bretton Woods, 29
Sise Inn, Portsmouth, 31

222

New Jersey
Bernardsville Public Library, Bernardsville, 32
Ringwood Manor, Ringwood, 35
Southern Mansion Inn, Cape May, 34
Van Wickle House, Somerset, 36

New Mexico
La Posada de Santa Fe Resort and Spa, Santa Fe, 207
Lodge Resort and Spa, The, Cloudcroft, 205
Old Cuchillo Bar, Cuchillo, 206
St. James Hotel, Cimarron, 204

New York
Beardslee Castle, Little Falls, 38
Belhurst Castle, Geneva, 37
Merchant's House Museum, New York, 40
Morris-Jumel Mansion, New York, 39
Seneca Falls Historical Society Museum, Seneca Falls, 41
Skene Manor, Whitehall, 42

North Carolina
Biltmore Village Inn, Asheville, 91
Duke Mansion, Charlotte, 93
Hammock House, Beaufort, 92
Mordecai House, Raleigh, 94

North Dakota
Sage Hill Bed and Breakfast/Country Inn, Anamoose, 156

Ohio
Buxton Inn, Granville, 160
Chateau Laroche, the Historic Loveland Castle, Loveland, 161
Franklin Castle Club, Cleveland, 157
Kelton House Museum and Garden, Columbus, 159
Squire's Castle, Willoughby Hills, 163

Oklahoma
Gilcrease Museum, Tulsa, 96
Stone Lion Inn, Guthrie, 95

Oregon
Chateau at the Oregon Caves, The, Cave Junction, 208
Heceta Head Light Keeper's House, Yachats, 212
McLoughlin House, Oregon City, 209
White Eagle Saloon, Portland, 211

Pennsylvania
Baker Mansion, Altoona, 44
Farnsworth House Inn, Gettysburg, 46
Harmony Inn, Harmony, 48
Jennie Wade House, Gettysburg, 45
Powel House, Philadelphia, 49

Rhode Island
Belcourt Castle, Newport, 52
Castle Hill Inn and Resort, Newport, 51
Sprague Mansion, Cranston, 50

South Carolina
Battery Carriage House Inn, Charleston, 98
Meeting Street Inn, Charleston, 100
Poogan's Porch Restaurant, Charleston, 99

South Dakota
Bullock Hotel, Deadwood, 165
Dakota Dream Bed and Breakfast, A, Hot Springs, 167
Historic Adams House, Deadwood, 164

Tennessee
Bell Witch Cave and Bell Cabin, Adams, 102
Belmont Mansion, Nashville, 104
Carnton Plantation, Franklin, 103
The Hermitage, Nashville, 105

Texas
Ashton Villa, Galveston, 107
Catfish Plantation Restaurant, Waxahachie, 109
Miss Molly's Hotel, Fort Worth, 106

Utah
Brigham Young Farmhouse, Salt Lake City, 214
Mary Fielding Smith House, Salt Lake City, 213
McCune Mansion, Salt Lake City, 215

Vermont
Equinox Resort, Manchester Village, 53
Green Mountain Inn, Stowe, 55
Hartness House Inn, Springfield, 54
Old Stagecoach Inn Bed and Breakfast, Waterbury, 56
White House Inn, Wilmington, 58

STATE INDEX

Virginia
Adam Thoroughgood House, Virginia Beach, 113
Berkeley Plantation, Charles City, 110
George Wythe House, Williamsburg, 116
Glencoe Inn, Portsmouth, 112
Kenmore Plantation, Fredericksburg, 111
Moore House, Yorktown, 117
Nelson House, Yorktown, 118
Peyton Randolph House, Williamsburg, 114

Washington
Stanwood Hotel and Saloon, Stanwood, 217

West Virginia
Blennerhassett Mansion, Parkersburg, 121
Boreman Wheel House Restaurant, Parkersburg, 122
Federal Arsenal Guest House, Harpers Ferry, 119

Wisconsin
Brumder Mansion, Milwaukee, 172
Galloway House and Village, Fond du Lac, 169
Hearthstone Historic House Museum, Appleton, 168
Historic 1856 Octagon House, Fond du Lac, 170
Taliesin, Spring Green, 171

Wyoming
Ferris Mansion Bed & Breakfast, Rawlins, 218
Trail End Historic Site, Sheridan, 219

NAME INDEX

Adam Thoroughgood House, 113
Amstel House, 12
Artist House, The, 68
Ashland, the Henry Clay Estate, 77
Ashton Villa, 107

Baker Mansion, 44
Battery Carriage House Inn, 98
Beardslee Castle, 38
Beauregard-Keyes House, 82
Belcourt Castle, 52
Belhurst Castle, 37
Bellevue Hall, 13
Bell Witch Cave and Bell Cabin, 102
Belmont Mansion, 104
Benton House Museum, 9
Berkeley Plantation, 110
Bernardsville Public Library, 32
Beverly Unitarian Church, 125
Biltmore Village Inn, 91
BJ's Bayou Restaurant, 193
Black American West Museum, 189
Blennerhassett Mansion, 121
Bliss Mansion, 199
Boreman Wheel House Restaurant, 122
Bowers Harbor Inn, 142
Brantley Mansion, 198
Brigham Young Farmhouse, 214
Brown Mansion, 137
Brownville Historical Society, 153
Brucemore, 133
Brumder Mansion, 172
Buford House Bed and Breakfast, 181
Bullock Hotel, 165
Buxton Inn, 160

Captain Fairfield Inn, 18
Captain Lord Mansion, 19
Carnton Plantation, 103
Casey Moore's Oyster House, 180
Castle Hill Inn and Resort, 51
Catfish Plantation Restaurant, 109
Cedar Grove Mansion Inn and Restaurant, 88
Chateau at the Oregon Caves, The, 208
Chateau Laroche, the Historic Loveland Castle, 161
Columns Hotel, 83
Copper King Mansion, 196
Country Tavern Restaurant and Pub, 30

Culver House, 127
Dakota Dream Bed and Breakfast, A, 167
Drish Mansion, 63
Duke Mansion, 93
DuPont Mansion Bed and Breakfast, 79

Equinox Resort, 53
Ernest Hemingway Home and Museum, 69
Errolton, 87

Farnsworth House Inn, 46
Federal Arsenal Guest House, 119
Felt Estate, 140
Ferris Mansion Bed & Breakfast, 218
Forepaugh's Restaurant, 145
Fort Sidney Museum and Post Commander's Home, 154
Franklin Castle Club, 157

Gaineswood, 61
Galloway House and Village, 169
George Wythe House, 116
Gibbs Museum of Pioneer and Dakotah Life, 147
Gilcrease Museum, 96
Glencoe Inn, 112
Glensheen, the Historic Congdon Estate, 143
Glessner House Museum, 126
Gold Hill Hotel, 203
Grant-Humphreys Mansion, 190
Green Mountain Inn, 55

Hacienda Mexican Restaurant, 132
Hammock House, 92
Hammond Castle Museum, 28
Hampton National Historic Site, 23
Hannah House, 131
Harmony Inn, 48
Harry S. Truman National Historic Site, 148
Hartness House Inn, 54
Hay House, 72
Hearthstone Historic House Museum, 168
Heceta Head Light Keeper's House, 212
Herlong Mansion Historic Inn and Gardens, 70
Hermitage, The, 105
Hernando Heritage Museum, 67
Higginson Book Company, 26
Historic Adams House, 164

NAME INDEX

Historic 1856 Octagon House, 170
Hotel Meade, 197

Iolani Palace, 192

James Farm, 149
Jameson Saloon and Inn, 194
James Stuart Cain House, 182
Jennie Wade House, 45
Jesse Lee Home, 177
Juliette Gordon Low Birthplace, 75

Kehoe House, 74
Kelton House Museum and Garden, 159
Kenmore Plantation, 111
Kennebunk Inn, 17

Lalarie House, 84
La Maison Guibourd-Valle, 150
La Posada de Santa Fe Resort and Spa, 207
LeDuc Historic Estate, 144
Lemp Mansion, 151
Liberty Hall Historic Site, 76
Lighthouse Inn, 7
Lizzie Borden Bed and Breakfast/Museum, 25
Lodge Resort and Spa, The, 205
Loudon House, 78

Mackay Mansion, 202
Madrona Manor Wine Country Inn and Restaurant, 183
Mary Fielding Smith House, 213
Mathias Ham House, 134
McCune Mansion, 215
McLoughlin House, 209
McRaven Tour Home, 89
Meeting Street Inn, 100
Merchant's House Museum, 40
Metro Salon and Day Spa, 201
Middleton Tavern, 20
Miss Molly's Hotel, 106
Molly Brown House Museum, 188
Monte Cristo Cottage Museum, 8
Moore House, 117
Mordecai House, 94
Morris-Jumel Mansion, 39
Mount Washington Resort, 29
Myrtles Plantation, 85

National House Inn Bed and Breakfast, 141
Nelson House, 118
Nevada Governor's Mansion, 200
Noah Webster House, 10
Nob Hill Inn, 186

Octagon Museum, 14
Ogallala Mansion on the Hill, 155

Old Cuchillo Bar, 206
Olde Pink House Restaurant, 73
Old Sheriff's House and Jail, 130
Old Slave House Museum, 128
Old Stagecoach Inn Bed and Breakfast, 56
Oliver House Bed and Breakfast, 178

Peel Mansion Museum and Garden, 65
Peyton Randolph House, 114
Poogan's Porch Restaurant, 99
Porter-Phelps-Huntington Museum, 24
Powel House, 49

Ringwood Manor, 35
Riordan Mansion State Historic Park, 179
Rosemont Museum, 191

Sage Hill Bed and Breakfast/Country Inn, 156
St. James Hotel, 204
Sauer Castle, 138
Schifferstadt Architectural Museum, 22
Seneca Falls Historical Society Museum, 41
Sise Inn, 31
Skene Manor, 42
Southern Mansion Inn, 34
Southgate House, 80
Sprague Mansion, 50
Squire's Castle, 163
Stanwood Hotel and Saloon, 217
Stokes Restaurant and Bar, 183
Stone Lion Inn, 95
Strawberry Hill Museum, 139
Sturdivant Hall, 62
Surratt House Museum, 21

Talcott House Bed and Breakfast, 10
Taliesin, 171
T'Freres Bed and Breakfast, 81
Trail End Historic Site, 219
Tuck U Inn at Glick Mansion, 136

Van Wickle House, 36
Victoria, The, 61
Villisca Ax Murder House, 135
Vino's Brewpub, 66
Voorhies Castle, 129

Warren House, 71
Waverly Mansion, 90
Whaley House Museum, 185
White Eagle Saloon, 211
White House, The, 15
White House Inn, 58
Winchester Mystery House, 187
Woodburn, the Home of Delaware's Governor, 11

Also available

The Big Book of Pennsylvania Ghost Stories
by Mark Nesbitt & Patty A. Wilson • *978-0-8117-0364-2*

The Big Book of Illinois Ghost Stories
by Troy Taylor • *978-0-8117-0504-2*

The Big Book of New York Ghost Stories
by Cheri Revai • *978-0-8117-0455-7*

Coming soon ...

The Big Book of Virginia Ghost Stories
by L. B. Taylor Jr. • *978-0-8117-0583-7*

The Big Book of Maryland Ghost Stories
by Ed Okonowicz • *978-0-8117-0561-5*

WWW.STACKPOLEBOOKS.COM
1-800-732-3669